MW00625818

Advanced Reviews

"For 130 years the *AFRO* has continued the choice work established by its founder, John Henry Murphy Sr., to be the voice of good news in the African American community, at a time when many people couldn't even read it. Into a contemporary minute of that ongoing momentum arises the voice of Dr. Kaye, who will not be silenced. Not ever. She brings to the community the ever-sounding alarm, "Injustice over here," and she does it with historical acumen and spiritual determination. She is a perfect complement to the message of America's Black Media Authority."

— Rev. Dorothy S. Boulware, *AFRO* Special Projects Editor

"Dr. Kaye Whitehead has dedicated her career to telling the stories of those who have not had the opportunity to do so themselves and using these stories as a tool to educate our community with the goal of facilitating understanding and allyship. In My Mother's Tomorrow, Dr. Kaye tells an authentic story of African American survival and strength through the eyes of those living in Baltimore's forgotten neighborhoods. The stories encapsulate what it means to live in a world where our concerns about violence and attacks on our community significantly outweigh our pursuit of joy, love, and excellence, creating a cycle of trauma. I proudly stand with Dr. Kaye in her persistent efforts to continue these important conversations about the obstacles that Black Americans face every day and work together to find ways to move forward in a way that works for everyone, not just a select few."

— Al Hutchinson, President & CEO, Visit Baltimore

"From the first time I read Dr. Kaye, it was clear that her voice was a force to be reckoned with. And as her first editor at the *AFRO* what was also clear is that she kept getting better as a writer and thought leader every time she delivered her often soul-searing columns. Each week she kept asking tough questions and kept delivering hard, clear-eyed answers for a community confronted with colossal challenges. Black people in America in many ways are facing unprecedented times: a 21st-century Civil War, a re-invigorated White nationalism, an attack on women, especially Women of Color, and a burgeoning fascism in American politics. Dr. Kaye confronts these challenges with power, passion and great intelligence. We need her voice.

    — Sean Yoes, author, documentary filmmaker, and former
      AFRO Baltimore Editor

my mother's tomorrow

dispatches through the lens of Baltimore's Black Butterfly

karsonya wise whitehead

Apprentice
House Press
Loyola University Maryland

Copyright © 2023 by Karsonya Wise Whitehead

All rights reserved. No part of this book may be reproduced or transmitted in any form or by any means, electronic or mechanical, including photocopy, recording, or any information storage and retrieval system, without prior permission from the publisher (except by reviewers who may quote brief passages).

This is a work of fiction. Names, characters, businesses, places, events and incidents in this book are either the product of the author's imagination or used in a fictitious manner. Any resemblance to actual persons, living or dead, or actual events is purely coincidental.

First Edition

Casebound ISBN: 978-1-62720-487-3
Paperback ISBN: 978-1-62720-488-0
Ebook ISBN: 978-1-62720-489-7

Printed in the United States of America

Design by Maria D'Agostino

Published by Apprentice House Press

Apprentice
House Press
Loyola University Maryland

Apprentice House Press
Loyola University Maryland
4501 N. Charles Street
Baltimore, MD 21210
410.617.5265
www.ApprenticeHouse.com
info@ApprenticeHouse.com

Six years ago, long before COVID, someone called my radio show (Today With Dr. Kaye on WEAA, 88.9 FM) and challenged me to go into The Black Butterfly neighborhoods and listen. He told me that there were stories to be told in Baltimore, but that people weren't listening. So I did. I walked and talked and listened. And then I wrote it all down. This book is for them. And for my husband Johnnie, my sons Kofi Elijah and Amir Elisha, and my daughter Mercedes Alexandria.

Nana said, Do the work for the children of your children.
I hope she knows that I am trying.

My mother is from Olar, South Carolina
My daddy is from Lexington
She puts salt on her watermelon
He says that he is a Geechee and
that he loves my mom despite this one watermelon flaw
I hate salt on my watermelon
I would have hated it even if
my daddy had not named me after him
He raised me to fight dragons and shadows,
To fall on my back, looking up, so I can get up
Mom says the bitter salt brings out the sweetness
And no matter the hurt, No matter the pain,
No matter No matter
Just use the bitter to bring out the sweet,
Use the laughter to even out the tears,
Use my pen to bring balance to my world
I am my father's yesterday
My mother's tomorrow
And my sons right now
Geechee once removed, I try to carry it all
I learned yesterday that I did not have to

Front cover credit: My mother and me, October 1968, Lexington, South Carolina

Contents

Acknowledgments

In 2017, during the first season of my radio show, *Today With Dr. Kaye*, someone called the show and told me that if I did not become intimately familiar with Baltimore's *Black Butterfly* neighborhoods, I would never understand Baltimore. He said that Baltimore had a rhythm, a pulse, and the only way to understand it was to immerse yourself in it. "Dr. Kaye," he said, "you must become a part of it, or you will always be an outsider. You have to meet the people and hear their stories. They are talking but nobody is listening." I took his advice seriously because I wanted to know and understand Baltimore. It is such a beautiful, complicated city. I moved here with my family 20 years ago and I am still discovering what makes it move. My sons, having grown up this city, are part of the soil and they understand it in ways that I never will. This is their home, but this is only where I live. There is, as they frequently remind me, a difference, subtle though it may be. So, I started visiting the neighborhoods in *The Black Butterfly*. I walked around them. I met the residents, and I listened to their stories. And with their permission, I shared them in a bi-monthly column in the *AFRO*. This book and my work on the radio to draw attention to their lives is for them.

The road to finishing a book is long and winding. It takes stamina, good people, and healthy snacks to help you reach the end. The Apprentice House's Maria D'Agostino prepared the first draft, which was then completed by Kevin Atticks, the Director of the Apprentice House, and Maryland's Secretary of Agriculture.

My Emmy-Award-winning radio show producer Justina Pollard-Bullock assisted me in producing shows that gave me the space to explore and share some of the stories and topics. The bi-monthly columns were edited by AFRO editors Sean Yoes, who helped me to think through the column when it first launched, and Dorothy Boulware, who helped me to think about topics that expanded beyond Baltimore and addressed some of the issues that Black communities were dealing with around the country. The final draft was copy edited by Ron Harrison, whose red pen and attention to detail kept me from straying too far from the stories that I was trying to tell. Any errant errors are, of course, all mine.

I also have a village of people who believe in me and support my work. Some of whom I know by name: O'Neal and Lajuana Johnson, Stephen and Kenya Duval, Stephanie and Best Davis, Dean La Vonne Neal and the Nealites, Courtney Carroll, Father Tim Brown, Charles Robinson, Travis Mitchell, Rev. Van Gayton, Billy Murphy, Esq; and so many more from my radio show *Today With Dr. Kaye*, Facebook, and Twitter that I do not. I thank them for their cheers, their criticism, and their gentle prodding, pushing, and poking along the way. This book is also for my siblings by birth and by marriage, my parents—who raised me to believe that a better world is possible and is on the way and for my children Mercedes Alexandria, Kofi Elijah, and Amir Elisha—who learned the hard way how to live with a Mother who wields her pen as a weapon and her paper as a shield.

And as always, every project I do is for and with my husband and best friend, Johnnie.

karsonya wise whitehead
Baltimore 6/23

I speak for the unforgotten

Baltimore City, like most urban spaces, has a particular type of rhythm. It has a pulse. It moves, and it breathes. It is a city that has grown despite the challenges. We are a microcosm of America, from *The Black Butterfly* to *The White L.* Lawrence Brown, in his book, *The Black Butterfly: The Harmful Politics of Race and Space in America,* describes *The Black Butterfly as "a geographic cluster of where Black Baltimoreans live and where capital is denied, and structural disadvantages accumulate due to a lack of capital access." The White L is where White folks live, enjoy, and capitalize off of their privilege and access.* In the midst of this reality, it is hard to stand up straight in the face of a country and a city that is counting on Black people to focus more on surviving than on thriving; more on not getting shot than on finding joy; and more on teaching our children how to get low and stay out of the way than how to dream out loud. On more days than I care to admit, this is how I feel living in America and how I feel living in Baltimore City.

Last night—once my house had settled down and the creaking had stopped, after everyone was done laughing and sharing, when a peaceful silence hung quietly in the air—I got up and walked through my house to check on my sons. This has always been the most peaceful moment of my day because it is during these moments that I know that my sons were home, and they were safe. Over the years, with the launch of Black Lives Matter, I would sometimes sit outside of their door, holding my head in my hand, trying to think about what I could do to help carve out a world and reshape a city where my sons could get home safe. It was frustrating for me because, as a mom and a professor and now the host of a daily radio show in Baltimore City, I live in a place of immense contradictions. I both love the city and am always frustrated by it. I write about the city, teach about the city, talk about the city, all the while trying to navigate and negotiate life, in and around the city. Baltimore is the type of place that keeps you up at night, tossing and turning, while trying to figure out what can be done to save it. There are so many questions and problems and challenges that need to be addressed that it sometimes feels like there is a deliberate plan in place to keep us from moving forward. The problem for me is that I am a pessimistic person. I have spent too many nights crying over the senseless killings in and around our city. I have watched with alarm the rising homicide numbers as Baltimore City has increasingly become more dangerous, more hostile, and more frightening. The pain in this city is palpable, and when my listeners call to share their lives and stories with me, it is hard for me not to lean in, not to react, and sometimes not to cry. There are days when I read through the news, and I wonder how we are going to survive and make it. I think about what it means to live in a city that is deeply segregated and economically separated and to try and exist within this space.

At the same time, Baltimore is also a city of incredible joy and resilience that always finds a way to move forward. There are days when I move around this city, heading down to have coffee at Nancy by Snac or take my sons to The Enoch Pratt Library, when I am absolutely convinced that Baltimore will outlive and outperform both my most significant concerns and my deepest expectations. I am in love with this city and marvel at the beautiful neighborhoods and the people, its history and its great potentiality, the nooks and crannies, the dents and the scratches that make up this place that I call home. I love the way that we rally and fight back against who does not see us, does not understand us, and does not recognize our incredible strength. That is the first lesson I learned about this city; they (now we) never give up.

In 2017, I began an in-depth ethnographic study within *The Black Butterfly* neighborhoods that were published in a monthly column in the *AFRO* newspaper. I chose the *AFRO* because it is the only newspaper that my daddy had delivered to the house. Established in 1892, the *AFRO* is the longest-running Black family-owned newspaper in the United States. When I started my study, I spent the day in the neighborhoods, talking to the residents, and documenting and recording their stories. When I visited the Poe Homes Community, in 2019, the residents were amid a water crisis and had gone four days without running water. They were spending their days filling up their buckets and pots from the fire hydrant so that they could drink it, bathe in it, and use it to flush their toilets. It was painful to watch, and it shook me to my core and made me question who we are as a city and who we want to become. As I walked through the neighborhood, I met a woman and talked to her as she was filling her pots and pans. She told me that she had stayed home from work all week because she did not have enough water for her and her children to both bathe and flush the toilet. She asked me, in a quiet but firm voice, "The Mayor, our Councilman, they don't see us. Baltimore City is a big place, so I think they just forgot about us. Is there any way that you can make us unforgotten?" I think about her often and about what it means to speak and write for those who are in a space where they cannot speak and write for themselves. I think about what it means to speak for those who believe that they have been forgotten, to document their stories and then share them, without judgment or malice. I share them because they matter.

It was painful, heartbreaking work as there are parts of Baltimore that have never recovered from the 1968 Riots. The people are hurting and are struggling to survive. Some of them were welcoming and friendly, delighted to talk and share; others were wary, suspicious, and, in a few cases, threatening. I spent almost three years collecting stories and sharing them in both print and on the radio. My goal, lofty as it was, was to recognize the rhythm of the neighborhood but not disrupt it. When I planned my first visit, I did it without having an inductive or deductive plan. I did not know how long it would take or where I would go. I only decided to venture out because one of my regular callers, James from Sandtown, challenged me to leave the radio studio and visit *The Black Butterfly* neighborhoods. "And don't just drive through," he said. "Get out of your car and walk around. Talk to the residents, visit the corner stores, and listen to the conversations. Get a real sense of how hard it is to live out here, on the edges of the city." I was once told that there are at least two Baltimores, separated by race and class. These are the edges of the city, and this is where my work started because even though our city is troubled and challenged, we will survive, and even if the world does not see us, we see each other.

stories of the forgotten

I will be the keeper of our stories.
I will be the keeper.
I will keep our stories.

Dear Black people

10/18/2019

For 400 years, we have tried to appeal to White America's humanity. We preached love and practiced non-violence even in the face of hatred and terror. We worked within their system, played by their rules, colored within their lines while desperately trying to prove our worth and convince them that we belonged here. We stood by and screamed, sometimes in silence and sometimes out loud, as they enslaved us, abused us, raped us, tortured us, and sold us. We have spent many years swallowing the lies that they have fed us and the injustice that they have meted out toward us. We were in the room when they legislated slavery, when they decided that we were three-fifths of a human, and when they chose to secede from the Union rather than set us free. The history of this country was written with our blood. We are the reason why America became America. We tilled the soil, raised the crops, tamed the underbrush, but we were not supposed to survive. Yet, we did not die. We are the descendants of men and women who chose survival as an act of rebellion.

Frederick Douglass, in 1851, argued that after 230 years of being chained and lashed, hunted with bloodhounds, and surrounded with utter insecurity. We had learned how to live on and how to smile under it all. We learned how to sing through our pain and laugh through our tears. And even when we thought we made it over, we were reminded time and time again that America—the land of the free and the home of the brave, the place that opens its arms to the poor huddled masses yearning to be free, the country that guarantees life, liberty, and the pursuit of happiness—had never been America to us. The reality is that for 400 years, we have been tormented, enslaved, and killed for the crime of being Black in America. We bore witness as they terrorized our neighborhoods, scared our children, violated our sisters, and incarcerated our brothers. We understood, even if we could not articulate it, that the only reason that White America stood tall was that they forced us to kneel so that they could stand on our backs. It was that way in the beginning, and it is that way today.

When the first 20 Africans arrived in this country, they showed us that Black lives, our lives, mattered. When our 10.6 million ancestors made it through the Middle Passage, ending up in the American South or in the Caribbean, they showed us that Black lives mattered. They mattered when slavery ended, and Jim Cow started; when the *Dred Scott* ruling said that we had no rights that the White man was bound to respect, and when the *Brown v. Board* ruling said that separate was not equal, equal was equal; and, when the Civil Rights Act of 1964 and the Voting Rights Act of 1965 were passed in Congress while Black men, women and children were being hosed and beaten in their community. They mattered when they killed our leaders, imprisoned our children, and redlined our communities. Our lives mattered. They mattered when Barack Obama was elected, and the full force of Whiteness, the one that we had witnessed with the rise of the KKK, was unleashed once more.

Black lives matter even when they try to tell us or show us that they do not. They matter even when they shoot us while we are on our knees, or while we are marching against oppression, or fighting against injustice. They matter when they lie and accuse our men and boys of rape and then respond by burning down our communities and beating and killing our people. They matter even when we are unarmed, and they shoot us while we are playing in the park or sitting in our own homes. Black lives, our lives, matter. Four hundred years later, and we are still trying to prove to White America that our lives matter.

Sit with that for a moment.

And then get angry with us because we built this country. We tilled the soil, raised the crops, and tamed the underbrush. Our blood is mixed with the soil of this land, and until Black lives matter, for Atatiana Jefferson, for Botham Jean, for all of us, then America—in all her shame and glory—will never be America.

And everybody knows about Baltimore, got dam

2/10/2022

In 1967, in a speech at Barratt Junior High School in Philadelphia, Dr. Martin Luther King Jr. asked the students, "What is in your life's blueprint?" He told them that the decisions they made on that day would determine how they would go forward and how we (as a community) would go forward. You, he explained, must decide on your blueprint, but it must be built on the work that others had done before you and must be able to be used by those who would come after you. My father would say something similar whenever I began to lose my way. He would sit me down and remind me that my life was meant to answer a question the world had been asking and waiting for me to answer. He would then tell me that his job was to spark my genius, set me on fire and then set me loose into the world so that my life would provide that answer. What are you seeking at this moment? Who are you supposed to be? What is the question that you are trying to answer? I wonder, in these moments, as I look around at the flames that are being extinguished in the hearts of the young people in this city, whether their genius is being sparked; whether they are being told that they are the ones that we have been waiting for; whether they are being challenged to be the answer to the questions that we hold in our heart. I wonder quite simply if Baltimore is failing its children.

In 1963, after the murder of Medgar Evers and the bombing of the Sixteenth Street Baptist Church, Nina Simone, in an act of rage, resistance and grief, wrote, "Alabama's gotten me so upset/ Tennessee made me lose my rest/And everybody knows about Mississippi Goddam." Someone said that at that moment, she weaponized music. As I look around Baltimore City, after recording 40 homicides in the first 38 days of 2022 and after ending 2021 with 300+ murders for seven years in a row, I know exactly how she felt and what she meant. *Baltimore Got dam, hold your hat because here we go again.* Violence on top of violence on top of violence. We are amid a racial and economic weathering. We are dealing with the result of years of injustice, underdevelopment, and miseducation. We are reaping what was sown by the seeds of White supremacy in this city. We are shadows walking through the haunted remains of someone else's dreams for our reality. And it hurts. It hurts like hell. Last year, I walked around with questions about freedom and justice, salvation and sacrifice, violence and pain, love and survival. In 2022, I want answers. We are at a moment, when our sheroes and heroes are dying, while people who are committed to eating us alive have both gained and remained in power. These are indeed the worst of times, but we must cry out like those who have cried out before us. We must protest. We must push back. We must love our children, believe in them, and move them to write the blueprint, to be the answer, to be better. I know that we are exhausted, but when we are individually weak, we are collectively stronger. It is when we send up the prayers that the blessings come down. And in the spirit of my praying grandmothers and here in the midst of Black History Month:

I pray for freedom: remembering the heroes and sheroes of our country and our movement who fought and gave their lives so we may have and appreciate and enjoy and defend our freedom.

I pray for justice: remembering the groups of people around the world who are not yet free and who do not yet have justice but continue to struggle for their freedom.

I pray for your tongue: remembering the age-old adage that they cut out our tongues to deny us the place to speak, so we sang from our souls and with our entire being.

I pray for Baltimore: remembering that we are all connected. We are all related that as we move forward, we stand on the shoulders of those who came before us, those who died for us, those who struggle with us, and we are the shoulders for those who are coming next, the ones that we hope will save us.

Finally, I pray for you: urging you to remember to pray for yourself. Pray for what you feel holds you back and ties you down. And then take a moment and pray for what sets you free, remembering that no matter how you define freedom, to get to the other side, we must pull up our anchors, fix our eye on something that we only see in our dreams, and believe that despite what they tell us, no matter how they limit us, our faith/our talents/our voices/ our strength will set us free and keep us on course.

What to a Black mother is your Fourth of July?

6/25/2021

You will never know real fear until you have that moment, the one when you give your Black son the keys to his first car, and he says, "Tell me again what to do when the cops stop me so that they don't shoot me." Somewhere, deep within me, I realized that he said "when" and not "if": when means it is going to happen; when means that it is inevitable; when means that he understands that he is a Black man in a White world; when means that he listened as I prayed for the mother of Philando Castile, of Miriam Casey, of Andrew Brown Jr., of Daunte Wright; when means that he understands that as a Black person, he is 20 percent more likely to be stopped, searched, cited, and arrested than White drivers; when means that he gets it; and it means that America, the land of the free and the home of the brave, has failed him.

Tell me again what to do…

When he was in high school, after watching all of his White friends get their licenses and then get a car, my son believed that having a car was a ticket to freedom. "You can go where you want," he would laugh and say, "when you want and for as long as you want. I get a car, and I'm going to be free." How do you tell your son that the pursuit of freedom has been the singular goal of Black people ever since we were kidnapped and dragged into this experiment that one day would be called democracy? We walked out of the Door of No Return, or off Gorée Island, or away from Kunta Kinteh Island and we planned and prayed for freedom. We stood on the auction blocks, being poked and prodded, barely understanding the foreign tongue that was negotiating our price, and we planned and prayed for freedom. We fought back as they tried to break us by raping, torturing, and terrorizing us, and we planned and prayed for freedom. We helped some to run, others to stay alive while we planned and prayed for freedom. We stood up and demanded our freedom from lynching and Jim Crow, from disenfranchisement and domestic terror, from redlining and economic injustice, from the mass industrial prison complex and discrimination, from police brutality and racial hatred, from White supremacy and Whiteness. We have been willing to die for our freedom even as we planned and prayed. So, how do I explain to my son that in America, freedom for Black people, as A. Philip Randolph once said, is never given; it is won. And freedom, as Medgar Evers said, has never been free.

When, I heard him say, *not if...*

This is why Juneteenth is complicated and why celebrating the Fourth of July as a day of American independence should never happen. In 1776, when White America celebrated its hard-won freedom from British rule, they did so while enslaving Black men, women, and children. It takes a certain kind of wickedness steeped in White supremacy to celebrate your country's freedom while simultaneously enslaving your countrymen and women. I feel comfortable using this familial term because, by that time, Black people had been in America for over 157 years and had died fighting for that freedom that White folks were enjoying. Six years earlier, Crispus Attucks, of African and Native American ancestry, was the first person killed in the American Revolution. And since that moment, Black people have been dying at the foot of the altar of Whiteness, fighting for our freedom. What to the Black mother—who has had her children pulled from her breast, has seen the soles of their feet hanging from trees, has watched them beaten and brutalized, has witnessed their abuse and degradation—is your Fourth of July? Nothing but a brutal reminder that our freedom will always be celebrated in the shadows if we let some White folks define it and define us.

I have been celebrating Juneteenth ever since I was a child. It was our day of freedom and independence. Even though we were in South Carolina and not in Texas, we would fire up the grill as my grandparents talked about freedom and the strength of our family. They embodied Black love and Black freedom. They talked about how the day was complicated because to accept that June 19th was a day of liberation and freedom for all Black people, you had to accept that Abraham Lincoln's Emancipation Proclamation ended slavery. And it did not. The Emancipation Proclamation only "ended" slavery within the Confederate States of America, a different country under the leadership of Jefferson Davis where Lincoln did not have the power to do so. They would get upset as they talked about how Lincoln chose not to end slavery in the states that he did control, so he could have ended slavery in Maryland or Missouri, in Delaware or Kentucky, but he did not. He was working to save the Union and not to free Black folks. Slavery, my grandfather would say, did not end with the Proclamation or when the South finally surrendered or even when soldiers reached Galveston Bay, Texas. It did not legally end until they ratified the 13th Amendment, and even then, and he would always sigh when he said this, we were free, but we didn't have our freedom. Talks of freedom never went well with burgers and boiled peanuts. I understood, even back then, the importance of celebrating Juneteenth as a moment of hope for our people without allowing the symbolism of the moment to replace the truth of what happened to us. I realized that we are more than the lies they tell us about ourselves.

When the cops stop me...

My son lives in Tennessee, down in the heart of the South, and when we handed him his keys on the eve of Juneteenth, less than two weeks from the Fourth of July, my heart stopped for just a moment. It was the When and not the If that got me. It was the realization that no matter how far we have come, we have so much farther to go. It was a moment within the spaces, between being free and having freedom, that made me catch my breath. If you are not Black in this country, then you will never know the very real fear that washes over you—like cold water on a sun-drenched day, like listening to your grandparents talk about freedom while sharing stories of White fear and Black death—until you give your Black son the keys to his first car and he says, "Tell me again what to do when the cops stop me so that they don't shoot me."

Yes, Baltimore is indeed on fire

11/21/2019

My Nana came and visited me in my dreams last night. She told me that I needed to imagine a world where justice exists and then fight like hell to make it happen. Although she died blind with cataract-stained eyes, in my dreams, she was able to see me. When I was younger, when she wanted me to listen to her, she would place both of her hands on the side of my face so that I could look her directly in the eyes. I knew that that meant that whatever she was saying was something serious, something I needed to hear. Something that she would ask me about later, so I always paid attention to what came next. She looked me in my eyes and quietly but firmly said, "They want to destroy us. They want to break us. They want us to burn. You have to pull our people back from the pit of Satan's hell." My Nana, even in death, is still finding ways to make me think about who I am and who I want to be. It is clear to me that at this moment, Baltimore is indeed on fire. We are being burned, and it feels like we are standing at the pit of hell. We are in desperate need of burnout. We need to set a controlled fire, point out, and burn the things that are destroying our community and do what we can to end this long night of despair. It is Dante's Inferno playing out in my life yet again.

I was a junior in high school the first time I read this book. My history teacher told us to read it in preparation for our field trip to the White House. Given that my history teacher was radical and fiery, I was not sure if we were going to be protesting the government or touring the building. He was a civil rights activist who had been arrested multiple times for civil disobedience and would often close the door during class, lower his voice, and ask us to think out loud about what we were willing to do to overthrow the system. He would post quotes by Martin Luther King and Karl Marx around the classroom and ask us to imagine a world devoid of capitalism, militarism, and racism; and, then to imagine what it would take to make this world possible. He assigned us passages from Mao's Little Red Book and made us question the efficacy of the Vietnam War, World War II, and Theodore Roosevelt's belief that one should **speak softly** and carry a big stick. He would stop by our table during lunch and ask us to think about what America would have been like if Dr. King had lived or if the South had won. He would encourage us to take sides and then walk off as we would begin to have vigorous and sometimes very loud and passionate debates. On that day, as we sat across the street from the White House, making protest signs, our teacher explained to us that we were living in Dante's Seventh Circle of Hell, the first ring of violence. It was, he said, because we were growing up in the "Murder Capital of the World," and we were being raised to see Black violence and Black death and Black anger as normal. We were being led to believe that people who looked like us were criminals and predisposed to violence. We were being taught that police brutality was a normal response to Black people because we needed to be policed and controlled. Images of Black depravity were inundating us, and we were not questioning this reality. We were on fire, and we did not even know it. As I sat in the grass, listening to my teacher rant and rave about politics and Reaganomics, about violence and Dante, I could not imagine another way of being. I had become comfortable with the fire, and like the characters in Plato's Theory of the Caves, I saw the fire and believed that it was real.

Much like the Washington, DC, of my childhood, Baltimore City is now in the first ring of the Seventh Circle of Hell, a place of suffering, where you are surrounded by and drowning in violence. It is overwhelming, and it feels like it will never end. It is depressing, and it hangs in the air. We are living during a time when everyday acts of violence are as commonplace as breathing (though, admittedly, there are days when it is hard to breathe in this city). Violence no longer moves us or interrupts our day. Young people in this city are struggling under the weight of continual traumatic stress disorder because violence has always marked and defined their lives. This year alone, we have seen a 30% increase in carjackings, a 20% increase in shootings, and we are on our way to hitting 300+ homicides for the fifth year in a row. Violence is not supposed to be normal. We are not predisposed to violence. We do not hate ourselves. It is a clear indication that our city is on fire, and the only way that we can stop the burning is to have a burnout. We need to set a controlled fire, point out, and burn the things that are destroying our community and do what we can to end this long night of despair. Yes, our city is on fire, but it can be saved. It can be rebuilt. It can be pulled back from the pit of hell, and then (and, only then) can it be free.

It's mourning time (again)

12/26/2019

Black folks, as my Nana used to say, must find a way to carve out their lives in the stitches. She would always talk about the system when she was knitting. She preferred circular needles to double-pointed ones; they were easier to hang on to whenever her hands moved faster than her mind could think. We are not allowed to mourn. We are not allowed to grieve. The system will do everything it can to make us believe that the death of Black people at the hands of other Black people is normal. She would sometimes stop in the middle of a sentence and look past me, but her hands, brown, beautiful, wrinkled, and strong, would never stop moving. Sometimes she would laugh or raise her voice or cry and drop her head, but her hands, they just kept moving. She was knitting and teaching and carving out her life in the stitches.

We do that right here in Baltimore City, where we carve out our lives in the stitches, the small cracks of light between the ever-present darkness. It is in the stitches, the little places within us, where we hold fast to both our love for this city and our hatred of the violence in this city. We know how it feels to grieve, to be doubled over in pain, gasping for air, unable to *squelch* either our tears or our moans. We know how to build makeshift memorials, how to burn sage, and how to keep going even when everything in us calls for us to stop.

We know how it feels to be knocked down, to be written off, to feel the boot—of persistent unemployment and systemic inequality, of redlining and lead poisoning, of broken promises and abandoned dreams—resting comfortably on our necks, holding us down. We have spent a lot of time on our knees, hands folded, heads bowed. We know how it feels to acknowledge that there are moments, in this city, where neither your voice nor your vote matters. (That Baltimore is top-heavy with Black faces only makes the sting even more significant.)

December 2019 has been a horrifically violent month in a horrifically violent year coming at the end of a horrifically violent decade.

For the past five years, Baltimore City has had over 300 homicides and has seen a rise in non-fatal shootings. This information, disturbing though it is, no longer shocks us or moves us or even stops us in our tracks. It now feels normal for this type of pain and trauma to exist in our city. My Nana, who was one of the first Black nurses in South Carolina, used to say that Black people did not have the luxury to mourn because our ability to be resilient was assumed. So, we burn candles. We say their names. We pray. This is our reality.

It is mourning time again in Baltimore, and we are once again standing at the edge between who we are and who we want to be. We take stock because there have been too many bullets and too many bodies. There have been too many broken campaign promises and too many scandals. We have had far too much pain, and we have become adept at burying our fear that our sons and daughters will not make it home at night.

We want to but are unable to disconnect, so we find ways to

bury our feelings. We hide the emptiness that is inside of us when we are called upon to bear witness to another mother's pain. We bury our anger and our fear when our leaders betray us, when they lie to us, and when they ignore us. We swallow our frustrations as we watch them care more about the few who have the most than the most who have the least.

In this city, we learned to follow the rules, to submit, to lower our chins, to shield our eyes, and to be still. We learned how to be invisible. We know what police brutality feels like, and we learned how to fight back. But whom do we fight when the person at the other end of the barrel looks like us? Whom do we fight when our brothers are killing our babies and killing our sons and daughters? In so many ways, it is not Baltimore City *at* war that scares me, but Baltimore City residents *at* war that keeps me up at night. As the mourning comes again into this city, bringing darkness into spaces where light once existed, I am no longer confident that we are going to survive what is happening here without being transmogrified, changed, scathed.

We stand face to face with ourselves, ending a decade that was once so full of promise and hope, where we choose to stand and hold our ground. We must find a way to knit ourselves together and share and shoulder our collective pain. We must find a way to be fully present for each other, to greet the dawn, exhale and dry our tears. We must find a way to bring the morning back to Baltimore, without our tears, without our blood, and without our mourning.

How to kick ass and hold on to the broken pieces

12/6/2019

I was raised by baby boomers, the last Jim Crow generation whose lives were shaped by the early days of the Civil Rights Movement, the words of Martin Luther King Jr., and the Vietnam War. They had been raised to believe that White people were not only better and smarter, but that they were also, in fact, closer to God. My parents said that even though they were never actually told that they were inferior, they were taught that White people were superior. As children, not one single person ever explained to them why they had to get on at the back of the bus or why they could never look White people in the eye. They never really understood the reasoning behind the separate water fountains and bathrooms or why they could never eat in the lovely restaurant downtown. They never wondered or questioned why they had to walk past brand-new schools, with playgrounds and manicured lawns, to get to a small dilapidated one-room shack where nothing was brand new, and everything was always broken. They grew up learning how to give way to Whiteness and how to swallow their anger. My father used to watch his father, and he noticed that whenever his father dealt with White men, he would lower his eyes while simultaneously throwing back his shoulders. It was those moments, when he watched his father practice subtle acts of resistance, that shaped who he was and helped him to find and claim his voice.

My parents were raised by the Silent Generation, traditionalists who were shaped by the Great Depression, World War II, and the frequent lynching of Black bodies by White hands. My grandparents believed that a world without Jim Crow was possible so that I would be able to look White people square in the eye while simultaneously throwing back my shoulders. My parents were taught that each generation is entangled in an inescapable network of mutuality, and it is their job to be a bridge for the next generation to walk over. They understood that their failures and their successes would mark the path that I would eventually tread. The moments where they fought and the moments where they relinquished determined how I navigated and negotiated this world. When my grandfather threw back his shoulders in the face of Whiteness, my father mimicked this gesture and then taught it to me. When my grandfather sang Negro spirituals, he taught my mother the words, and then she taught me the meaning. When my grandfather taught my father to pray, to fold his hands and wait for change to come, my father listened and then unfolded them, used them to dismantle a racist system, and forced change to happen.

When I was growing up, I used to spend every summer in South Carolina with my father's parents on their farm. I would run through their woods and sit down by the lake. I would take my journal and lie on a blanket and write about who I wanted to be when I grew up. My grandfather would always make his way down to the water after he finished his chores. I would know when he was coming because he used to sing. He had a deep baritone voice that would carry in the woods, and his singing would lift me up, would make me feel free, and would cause me to start singing as well. "The problem with White people," he would say as he sat down on the blanket and pulled out his chewing tobacco, "is that they want to take everything from you. It is not enough for us to hold onto even the broken pieces of ourselves; they want that from us, as well." He would rest for a moment, studying the water, chewing, and spitting. "I taught your Daddy how to hold on to his broken pieces; you need to learn how to do the same." My father said that when he used to march against Jim Crow, he would tell himself to hold on to his broken pieces, and when his family was being terrorized by the KKK, he would remind himself to hold on to his broken pieces. When he sent me off to college and graduate school, to Kenya, and then down the aisle to get married, he told me to hold on to my broken pieces. My parents are baby boomers, the last Jim Crow generation. They taught me how to kick ass, how to sing, how to survive Whiteness, and how to hold on to my broken pieces.

A tale of two cities

8/23/2019

For some of us, who live in Hamden or Mount Washington, the reality of having to set up No Shoot Zones where children can be safe from gun violence does not actually make sense. In that same vein, if you live in Fells Point or Hamilton, it is probably a little difficult to try and understand why it is so hard for people to adopt a 72-hour ceasefire and agree to not shoot anyone. But, for those of us who live inside the heart of Baltimore, in communities that are intimately connected to the already 186+ homicides we have had this year, we understand that with the increasingly high-stakes nature of survival and the ongoing work to change the culture of the inner city, all voices and ideas must be incorporated. They must be tried, and we must be stalwart in our attempt to move this city forward. It is an ongoing struggle, but every activist and parent and resident of this city must be committed to doing the work to develop solutions that advance racial, economic, and social liberatory possibilities for our marginalized communities. We are no longer able to live safely within our neighborhood silos because when one of our residents is suffering, we are all suffering.

The work to change this city is not new, but the solutions set forth by Tyree Colion from No Shoot Zones and Erricka

Bridgeford from the Baltimore Ceasefire are. Both Colion and Bridgeford draw heavily upon the work that has been developed by Leaders of a Beautiful Struggle, Safe Streets, Baltimore's Civil Rights Office, Ericka Alston's Kids Safe Zone, and Baltimore Bloc, to name just a few. It is their commitment to trying to unravel the racist economic threads that bind us so tightly to the past that gives me hope. These are the days when the light shines the brightest in this city. On other days, when you look around and see the crime and the depression and the pessimism, it is hard to fight against the feelings of frustration and anguish that come from confronting racial injustice and social inequality every single day of your life. It is hard sometimes to stand up straight in the face of a country and city that are counting on Black people to focus more on surviving than on thriving, more on not getting shot than on finding joy, and more on teaching our children how to get low and stay out of the way than how to dream out loud. On more days than I care to admit, this is how I feel living in America *writ large* and how I feel living in Baltimore City. In the wake of the recent Baltimore Ceasefire, I vacillated between feeling relieved with every hour that passed without a shooting and feeling depressed about knowing that I live in a city where death is the new normal. I think about it daily and to paraphrase Lin Manual Miranda, I imagine Black death and pain so much it feels just like a memory. It is overwhelming because when I look at the work of our Colion and Bridgeford, I know Baltimore City can and should do better. The problem, and this is a well-known fact, is that Baltimore embodies the tale of two cities. On any given day, depending upon whether you are in Mount Washington or Sandtown-Winchester, you are either in the best of times or the worst of times. You are dealing with either an epoch of belief about how much we can accomplish or an epoch of incredulity about how much pain we can deal with without completely falling apart. The city is racially and economically divided, and whether you thrive or survive is deeply tied to where you are born. In this city, where you are born and raised determines how long you are going to live and the quality of your life.

According to the Health Department, a child born in a neighborhood like Homeland or Roland Park can expect to live to the age of 84 while a child born in Clifton-Berea, where nearly one in three families live in impoverished homes, the life expectancy is around 60—two decades less. So even though we may live in the same city, a few blocks can make the difference between living and dying. It makes a difference because here in Baltimore, in the most economically challenged neighborhoods, children are exposed to higher levels of neighborhood violence, poor diet and nutrition, and an ongoing lack of proper medical care. They are living in war zones where they have a higher chance of being a victim of homicide, a higher chance of getting cancer and heart disease and a higher chance of being involved in a non-fatal shooting. They live beside rows of boarded-up houses in communities overrun with liquor and tobacco stores. Due to decades of redlining and economic underdevelopment, we have economically challenged all-Black neighborhoods with lackluster schools sitting only blocks away from robust, all-White neighborhoods with half-million-dollar homes and expensive private education. It is a deeply racially segregated city and system, and it helps to explain why No Shoot Zones and Ceasefire are not just wanted but they are needed. It is how we can comfortably reimagine our communities and work towards establishing liberated free and safe spaces for all of us. This is how we win. This is how we bend our privilege, and this is how we change our city.

You tell them that we're not invisible; you tell them that we matter

11/28/2019

For the past five months. I have spent my days driving around and visiting *The Black Butterfly* neighborhoods of Baltimore City. I visited the schools, the corner and liquor stores, and the churches. I rode the bus through the neighborhoods, listened in on some conversations, and talked to some of the residents. There were days when I was overwhelmed by the feelings of despair, the rows of boarded up houses, and the ever-growing piles of trash. There were days when I walked on some blocks, and it felt like time was standing still. The streets looked abandoned. The houses looked old almost as if the world had moved on and had forgotten that they existed. On my third week of walking around, an elderly woman, who reminded me of my grandmother, wanted to know what I was doing and why I kept showing up. She wanted to know if I was cop or if I was lost. I fumbled around for an answer. How do you tell someone that you are walking through their neighborhood so that you could bear witness to their suffering? I tried to explain that I was the host of "Today With Dr. Kaye" and that I wrote for the *AFRO* and that I wanted to document what was happening in our city. I knew that I was rambling and that I probably sounding like an outsider or an interloper, but I wanted her to understand why I was there and why I had to document what I saw. I also wanted her to understand why I kept coming back. She looked at me, long and hard, and then, as she turned to walk away, she said, "Dr. Kaye, we're invisible to them. They don't see us. They don't hear us. They don't care about us. You tell them that we're not invisible. Tell them that we matter."

> *Day 25: It is so hot out here. Kids are running around, pouring water on each other. I sat on the stoop of an abandoned house hoping that I wouldn't draw any attention to myself. The air feels different over here— sticky and heavy. There are no parks, no green spaces, no place for children to play so they run around on the sidewalk, darting in and out of traffic. My grandmother used to say that when you are poor, you carve your joy out in stitches by focusing only on the moment and finding a way to give thanks for that. My grandmother was poor and saw it as a badge of honor, rather than one of shame. She said that being poor made her strong, and strength is a blessing, not a burden. I am looking around for Miss Janet, maybe because she reminded me of my grandmother or maybe because I just need to see a friendly face…. I hope she is ok.*

I thought about Miss Janet and what she said every time I walked through her neighborhood. I used to look for her because I wanted her to know that I heard her. I wanted her to know that I saw her. I wanted her to know that she was not invisible to me. I have written this letter to her a dozen times in my mind, especially on the days when I watched the students walk through the snow and ice on their way to school. I have tried so hard to put words down on paper, especially on the days when I read about the increasing neighborhood violence or walked past another sidewalk vigil with candles and teddy bears and handwritten notes. I tried to write something on the day when I walked into one of the schools and saw the bars on the windows, the trash in the hallways, and our children, sitting in overcrowded classrooms trying to learn. I wanted to share her message with them, to let them know that they are not invisible and that their lives and their futures do matter. I understand Black invisibility in a city where politicians argue about policies and theories while their most vulnerable residents suffer in silence. I understand Black suffering and the reality of life in *The Black Butterfly* versus life in *The White L.* I understand this system is designed to keep you impoverished. It thrives on your suffering and breeds on your pain. I understand that you are living in a conflict zone within a stressful environment that causes severe, prolonged trauma.

> *Day 46: School is back in session, and it is as hot in the classrooms as it is outside. Probably hotter. Some teachers have complained that they have already run out of water and toilet paper. What type of school system allows their children, the most vulnerable population, to attend a school without water or breathable air? It is obvious that the children of those in power in this city do not attend these schools that are troubled and dysfunctional. Suffering is a burden that is only carried by the people who have the most need, who have the least amount of money, who receive the least amount of care and attention. If I were to grade this city on how they treat their children, then Baltimore City (and perhaps by extension, I) would fail because we are failing them.*

There were days when I got home from these neighborhoods, sat in a chair in my living room and cried. Those were the days when it took me a few hours to decompress, breathing slowing and talking myself through my pain. I did that after only a few hours of walking through these neighborhoods; I can only imagine what it must be like if you are unable to leave. What do you do when the most dangerous place that you can imagine is a place that you call home? Where do you go when you cannot afford to move and you cannot imagine another way forward? In your moments of pain and sorrow, whom can you count on to hear you, to see you? How do you deal with the everyday reality that comes from living in *The Black Butterfly* and dealing with Black invisibility and Black suffering? What do you do? I believe that you send up an emergency flare; you speak your pain into the wind, "You tell them that we are not invisible. Tell them we matter."

They tried to bury us; they didn't know we are seeds

10/25/2018

I believe that it is now fair to say that despite our best intentions—our marches and our calls for peace, our prayers, sage burning, and our moments of silence—Baltimore City is rapidly becoming an experiment in urban living that is going horribly wrong. Ever since the fallout from the 2015 Uprising, this city has become more violent, more deadly, and more frightening. In the past month alone, we have seen a rise in homicide numbers and a sharp uptick in the number of shootings, including 11 people being shot in one day and two dozen people being shot in less than a week. Our cultural milieu is reminiscent of the Wild West, a place without laws but with guns, lots and lots of guns. The Mayor believes that the city is amid a drug and turf war while I believe that this is what tends to happen in a Category Five, deeply segregated, poverty-stricken city without enough police officers or a health commissioners, and a history of predatory policing. There are communities in the city where the sounds of gunshots and police sirens have become so familiar that they are embedded in the cultural fabric that stitches the community together. We are in a dark sunken place in need of some encouragement and some hope.

Now, I may not have all the answers on how to turn this city around, but I can offer a little light. Baltimore City is a city of survivors and despite how grim it may look at this moment, I believe that no city has worked harder to push for equality and peace more loudly or with a stronger voice. No city in our recent history has sacrificed more to try to improve the lives of all. And I believe that there is no other city that deserves a win quite like we do. We must take a moment to breathe and to remember how far we have come and how much farther we must go. We must remember our foundation and our roots. We must remember that though they are trying to bury us under a narrative laced with stories of violence and destruction filtered through a lens of White supremacy, we are seeds and we will find a way to sprout and grow. We must remember how to fight and that we come from a long line of people who were willing to sacrifice and fight in order to save us and to save our communities.

Frederick Douglass once talked about what it would finally take for people to resist and fight. He stated that there comes a moment when people reach the end of their tolerance for injustice and mistreatment and that when that happens, they will resist with "either words or blows, or with both." I sometimes wonder if we (as a city) have reached that moment. Are we frustrated enough, angry enough, pissed off enough to want to fight to save this city? Are we willing to get out on the corners and into the faces of those who are destroying our community and force them to flee? How much longer are we willing to allow death to happen at our doorstep while we pretend that we do not see the bodies? Douglass knew that we needed to be the ones to fight for our freedom, to record our history, to tell our stories, to remind the world of who we were, and to show them what we have become. We need to be the ones to tell our young brothers and sisters (the ones who seemed to have lost their way) that the strength of our people and the strength of this city is uniquely tied to our ability to mobilize the best and the brightest. We must remember that even though our city has a myriad of challenges, we are standing on Holy Ground, in a country that has been built on our backs, that has survived because of our sacrifice, and that continues to be a place of greatness because of our brilliance. We must remind them.

It is time to reclaim our neighborhoods, reclaim our children, and reclaim the future that we have worked for hundreds of years to have in this country. We have to teach them a lesson about themselves, the one that America often fails to remember about Black people: that we are resilient and failure for us has never been an option; that we are brilliant and we can effectively mobilize the collective strength of our genius and strategically plan for a better tomorrow; that we are knitted together so that our collective strengths support our collective weaknesses; and, that we are always on the defense and have never stopped being on the lookout for those subtle shifts when the winds of oppression and degradation, of second-hand citizenship and destruction begin to blow once again in our direction. We must be the ones to save this city and we must remember, in the words of James Weldon Johnson, that despite what is happening in this city at this moment:

We will sing a song full of the faith that the dark past has taught us,

And We will sing a song full of the hope that the present has brought us,

And we will face the rising sun of our new day begun, And *Baltimore City* will march on till victory is won.

Let's tear some shit down in order to get free

11/7/2018

I am a Southern girl at heart. I spent my summers in Lexington County, South Carolina on a farm with an outhouse, miles of land, and a lake that sat at the bottom of the hill at the edge of my grandmother's property. She was a farmer and a fisherwoman, with a mane of blazing red hair and a personality that was almost too big to capture. She seemed to always be in motion, even when she was standing still. She used to spend her days sitting beside the water, silent, just waiting for something to happen. She said she could always tell when change was in the wind because she felt a stirring in her soul and an ache in her right hip. Whenever she talked about race relations, White supremacy, or poverty, she would say that there was a storm a-brewing in this here nation and once it settles, things are never going to be the same again.

For the past three years, ever since the Baltimore Uprising, I have been walking around this city with an ache in my hip and a stirring in my soul. I have had this growing sense that we were right on the edge of a revolution, that critical moment when unstoppable change begins to take place. I have spent many nights with one eye open in order to witness the reality of what happens in a city with unchecked violence and a growing distrust of police and politicians. A city where we talk and complain but we do not move. We hold our pearls and clutch our chests, but we do not march every single day. We pray and burn candles, but we do not disrupt the status quo. We are being herded but not led. We are being tolerated but not trusted. We are watching mini-cities get built with millionaire tax breaks, but we are not willing to, in the words of one of my former students, "tear some shit down in order to get free." I believe that we have reached that tipping point, and I am waiting for my people to rise up, ban together, and demand the change that we so rightly deserve. There is a storm a-brewing in this here city and once it settles, things are never going to be the same again. It is a storm of discontent, a storm of deep frustration, and a storm that bespeaks of a growing sense of resentment and malaise.

I wonder, are you as tired as I am of living in a city that is constantly put under the lens, watching all of the faults, missteps, and embarrassing moments get exposed to the world. From the photographs of our children freezing in their classrooms to reports of the criminals in the Gun Trace Task Force, from the crumbling infrastructure in our schools to the rising homicide numbers—we are always subject to America's gaze, always made to feel like we are the Black sheep of Maryland, the wayward child, the crazy uncle who can never seem to get his life together. The winds of change are quietly blowing through this city, and it is past time for good folks to rise up and get ready to tear some shit down so that we can save this city.

My grandmother taught me that there is a difference between a riot and a revolution, and I am actively calling for the latter and not the former. We know how to bring about change. It is as part of our DNA, both as a nation and as a people. We know how to protest. We know how to fight. And we know how to break the back of tyranny. In 1654, as the nation was still in the very early stages of growth and development, eleven enslaved men and women petitioned for, and won, their freedom and land from the council of New Netherland (New York). This was one of the first documented Black protests in America. Since then, Black people have continued to be involved in an ongoing struggle to achieve either freedom or equality or, in some instances, both. Within our community, the question was (and is) never *if* we should get involved in the struggle for civil rights and civil liberties, but rather, when, where, and to what extent. We know what it feels like to be free and what it means to save our communities. We have seen this country advance—from its early days as a young nation to its current role as a world power—and we have contributed to it but have not always been able to benefit from it. The political and social mores that make up this country also define who we are in this country, so struggle is not new to us. The storm that is a-brewing should feel familiar. It happened in the courtroom in 1849, with the *Roberts v. City of Boston* case, as lawyers argued that legalized segregation psychologically damaged Black students; and on the streetcars in 1867 when Caroline Le Count, a freeborn educated woman, engaged in civil disobedience to force the city to enforce the law that integrated public transportation. It happened in 1851 when Sojourner Truth, at the Akron Convention, challenged a committee of men to think about the rights of women and again one year later when Frederick Douglass challenged Americans to think about the significance of the Fourth of July in the lives and the experiences of enslaved and formerly enslaved Black people. It happened in 2015 when Baltimore City rose up and demanded justice for Freddie Grey, and it happens every Wednesday when the family of Tyrone West stands up and demands justice for him. This ongoing movement for justice and equality have defined who we are. Struggle is what we do, and we do it well. Baltimore, this is our moment, when we must decide what type of city we want to be and what type of future we want to carve for our children. If we continue to let this city go down its current path, we will have nothing more to leave them but smoke, ashes, and stories of a lost generation that sat back and watched its city burn itself to the ground. There is a storm a-brewing in this here city and once it settles, things are never going to be the same again.

Is Baltimore City broken?

4/11/2019

Between Baltimore City and the rest of the world, there is always a hint of an unasked and therefore unanswered question. It is a question that is rooted in *anti-Blackness* and framed by years of deliberate Black oppression and suppression. It is a question that is difficult to ask of a city that seems to move from one scandal to the next without pausing for a moment to catch its collective breath. Outsiders look at us with a wary eye, head cocked, with the question ready on their lips. They are not sure of how to frame it, how to ask it without making us angry. They do not seem to understand that the very same question that they are afraid to ask is the same one that we ask of both our politicians and of ourselves all the time: Is Baltimore (our beloved city) broken beyond repair? We are a city full of dreamers, and we want—no, we deserve—to be seen and treated better. We are, as Robert Browning once wrote, a place where we desire for our collective reach to exceed our collective grasp. I think deeply about Baltimore City, about who we are and what we can become. I read our history and the stories about our city with one eye closed. This is an old lesson for me, one learned when I was in college, living abroad in Kenya with a blind woman in Chemundu. She knew that I was a history major, and she told me that I should always read the White man's version of my history with one eye closed because until the day comes when the hunted learn how to write, the stories would always center on the hunter.

Stories and articles about Baltimore City, our neighborhoods, and our residents, should be read with one eye closed. I remember this lesson fondly, and it is one of the reasons why I chose to conduct an in-depth ethnographic study of Baltimore's most economically challenged, hypersegregated neighborhoods. I wanted to write, record, and tell the stories of the people who live and reside on the margins of the margins. They are the most vulnerable. They are the most attacked. They are the ones who are dealing with the short- and long-term impact of continuous traumatic stress disorder, never-ending community violence, broken promises from elected officials, predatory and corrupt policing, and lead poisoning They send their children to schools with crumbling infrastructures, where decisions are made about them without having a conversation with them. Their stories need to be told and centered. They should be shared like the secret messages of freedom that were sent between the plantations and shared among the enslaved people to give them hope and encouragement. I think of the words of my colleague, Treva Lindsey, who said that White supremacy does not love us; therefore, we need to learn to love and love on each other hard. This is what my act of radical political love looks like—a little bit of hope being passed from one hand and heart to the next by telling their stories, hearing them speak, bearing witness to their pain, and believing out loud with them and in their story.

When I visit the communities, I tend to focus on the schools, talking to as many students as I can. I believe that young people are not just our future; they are our last line of defense. They can rewrite this world. Last week, I hosted a Teen Summit at the Academy of College and Career Exploration (it is in the

Hampden area, but the students come from South and East Baltimore), and I asked them whether Baltimore City was the place that they call home, broken beyond repair. This was my second conversation with them, and they had spent some time between my visits, thinking about Baltimore and about who they wanted to be in the world. De'Shawn spoke first and was clear in his assertion that Baltimore City is broken but not beyond repair: "We just need a lot of help, and we need those who are supposed to help to do the work and fix it." Tiaja chimed in and said that the problem is that the entire city is dangerous. "People are getting stabbed inside the schools," she said, "and then you can be in the wrong place at any time in this city and get shot. The people who are supposed to save us and protect us are not doing their job." They were just getting warmed up: "It is dangerous." "It is broken." "They don't care about us; they never did." Shanaya spoke up, "But we care about us, and we can repair it." We spent the next hour talking through the issues that this city is facing, from the state of the schools to community violence, from the mayor to the police force. I heard them. I saw them, and when I was packing up to go, Amir came over to me and said, "The first time you came I didn't think anything was going to change because we talk about the problems all the time; but you made us feel like we could change it. I don't remember what you said, but it's like you gave us hope."

Baltimore is my Beirut

1/23/2019

With the constant shifting narratives that seem to shape and define Baltimore City, there sometimes appears to be very little time to stop and ask the difficult questions. This is an ongoing challenge, but we as residents must be committed to carving out those moments when we can reflect on what is happening and why. It is only within those reflective moments that we can begin to imagine another way forward. Over the past weekend, as we celebrated the life and legacy of Martin Luther King Jr., eleven people were shot in this city. This is not shocking or surprising news: in fact, it is the assumed norm. We are expected to have multiple shootings. We are expected to be a dangerous city spinning out of control. We are expected to soldier forward as if this is the only reality that can exist. We are expected to accept the continued omission and erasure of our stories. Given that there is an implied dominant narrative—where the stories of violence and death and poverty are centered as if they are the norm—we (those of us who are conscious and who are working for change) must be willing to work to decenter that reality and then center our stories of survival.

We no longer have the option to wait as politicians and thought leaders spend more of their years and more of our money pondering possible directions and solutions. If we want this city to change, it is up to us to imagine a new way forward. It is with all of this in mind that I began my unofficial ethnographic study within *The Black Butterfly* neighborhoods of Baltimore City. I am well aware that there are two *Baltimores* and that the city is economically divided, but I believe that one of the ways to close the divide is for people to be willing to experience both parts of our city. It is not until you experience it for yourself—when you walk through the neighborhoods, visit the schools and churches, shop at the corner stores, talk to the residents and hear their stories—that you begin to get a sense of how much work needs to be done to tear down that barrier and bring this city together. I met Ray and Dave, two elderly gentlemen, in the Greater Mondawmin area. They both grew up in Edmondson Village and have never lived outside of the city. Ray told me that he was a veteran and that he remembered, in bits and pieces, what it was like to fight in a war and then come back home to Baltimore. "You commit your life to fight for this country," he said, "then you come back home and where you live is worse than where you were fighting. It's like the war never ended." "I got drafted too," Dave said. "I fought. I know a lot of people who died there; but right now, around here, this is like Beirut." They both started laughing; perhaps it was a type of gallows humor, but I found it difficult to join in. "Yea, that's right," Ray noted, "Baltimore is my Beirut." I asked them if they could remember a moment when the city and its narrative began to shift. I wanted to know when did Baltimore, the place of their childhood dreams and where they came of age, become this Baltimore. They started talking to each other, offering dates, agreeing, and disagreeing, finishing each other's sentences. "'68," Ray said. "It changed when King got killed." Dave nodded his head. "Yea, it ain't really been the same since then."

It was on April 6, 1968, two days after Dr. King was

assassinated, that Baltimore City found itself in the middle of an uprising. It began on Gay Street, after three hundred people had come together (peacefully) for a memorial service. In less than six hours, more than one thousand protestors had come out and started to fill the streets in East and West Baltimore. The city responded by banning sales of firearms and alcohol and declaring a state of emergency. Spiro Agnew, then Governor of Maryland, called in the National Guard and the Maryland State Police. Eight days later, six people were dead, 700 had been injured, 5800 people had been arrested, 1000 small businesses were damaged, and property damage was somewhere in the $12 million range. Although most of the damage was centralized in the neighborhoods where the protestors lived, it severely affected the city, and parts of Baltimore have never recovered. If, as Dr. King once wrote, riots are the language of the unheard, then during this time, Baltimore's inner city—which suffered from sub-par housing, high rates of infant mortality, drugs, gang violence, underemployment, and high unemployment rates—seems to be working hard to make its voice heard.

It has been almost fifty-one years, and if you walk around *The Black Butterfly*, talk to the residents, and listen to their stories, there is a growing sense that they believe that their voices are being silenced, their stories are being ignored, and their language is not being heard. "They keep saying that Baltimore is changing, that it's getting better," Dave said, "but from where I sit—" "Me too," Ray interrupted. "I'm sitting here too." Dave chuckled and then looked around the neighborhood, maybe at the sea of dilapidated houses or the trash on the sidewalk. Maybe he looked at the liquor stores or at the young boys standing on the corner. Or maybe he looked far beyond what my eye could see. He then shook his head and said, very quietly, "It's just not getting any better for us."

Black people, we need (a) threshing

7/31/2019

Growing up, I spent every summer on my grandmother's farm in South Carolina, and she would often use farming metaphors to teach me lessons. Every time a boy broke my heart, or I dealt with racism, she would tell me that it was time to do some threshing, which is the first step in sifting wheat. During the threshing process, the goal is to loosen the chaff from the edible grain. My grandmother did it the old-fashioned way when she spread out the wheat onto her stone floor, and she would beat it with a stick. It was hard back-breaking work, but it had to be done. It was a necessary step, she would say, to separate what was needed from what had to be discarded. She said that sometimes when things happened to us when things were holding us back from becoming the best of who we were supposed to be, we needed to be relentless, to act without emotion, and to separate what was needed from what had to be discarded or left behind.

This summer, it feels like Baltimore City desperately needs a threshing process as it is becoming painfully apparent that we need to separate what is needed to help move this city forward from the things (or people) that are holding us back. In the past two months alone, we have seen city shootings increase by 20%, a spike in our homicide numbers (we are on pace to reach 300+ for the fifth year in a row), a gnawing sense that there is a lack of police presence and involvement, a community that went without water for over a week, and an increase in teen crime and violence. Some residents genuinely believe that our elected officials have no concern about our *manque de bien-être.*

We need threshing, and though it will be backbreaking and hard, it is necessary. We live in a "no snitching" culture, either out of fear or out of loyalty. In either case, between no-snitching and the failure of the police to solve crimes (according to the Washington Post, approximately 65% of crimes in Baltimore go unsolved), we are at the threshing point. We are at a moment when we need to speak up when injustice and crime are happening, we need to hold our politicians and ourselves accountable, and we need to lean into the lives of some of the young people in this city who seem to be careening along a path toward destruction.

I believe that Baltimore City will survive, but I am not as optimistic as I used to be. I have seen too much suffering and pain in this city. I have watched, with despair, how it is increasingly becoming more dangerous, more hostile, and more frightening. There are days, and this is one of them when I look at the landscape of this city, and the challenges that we continue to face, and I wonder why—with all the smart and dedicated people that we elected—it feels like we are falling apart. I wonder if some of the leaders of this city understand what their responsibility is to us, their constituents. As elected officials, they are supposed to do more, to care more, to show up when our hearts are breaking, and when our neighborhoods are falling apart. They are supposed to be there when our children are scared and when our elders get robbed at gunpoint. They are supposed to see us, to take our calls and answer our messages, to help shoulder our burdens, and to speak for us when we are unable to speak for ourselves. They are supposed to be our beacons of light, illuminating a path that will move us forward from this seemingly never-ending cycle of poverty and crime and violence. They are supposed to be there on the first day when our entire community does not have any running water, or when the lights go out on our block, or when our community is in desperate need of a respite from the violence.

These are not new issues I discuss them almost every day on my radio show, and there are moments, like when Poe Homes was without water, or the teens attacked an older man, when I am not sure how we can go forward. I am not sure where we go from here or how we end the pain that is so evident in this city. I do not have any solutions; I just remember that when things were falling apart in my life and when it felt like I had lost control, my grandmother would say that it was time for threshing. Baltimore City, we need threshing, and though it will be hard back-breaking work, it must be done. It is a necessary step in which we separate what is needed to save us from what is destroying and killing us. Once we thresh, we will then start to winnow.

I'm from Baltimore;
I'm already dead

12/12/2018

At any given moment, there are about a half a million stories that need to be told about the reality of growing up and trying to grow old in Baltimore City. Stories about racial and economic inequality; about predatory policing and structural racism; about health disparities and food apartheid; about some of the people who died, like Freddie Grey and Tyrone West, Taylor Hayes and Wadell Tate; and about all the people who are trying to live. In the book of Acts, the apostle Paul tells his fellow shipmates that an angel told him that the ship was going to crash, and for them to survive, they would need to hang onto the broken pieces and make their way to shore. This is what it feels like trying to grow up and grow old in some neighborhoods in our city—you do everything you can to hang onto the broken pieces and try like hell to make it to the shore.

Life in Baltimore City is complicated. It is challenging and hard. It is racially segregated and economically divided. It is a tale of two cities—one mostly White and the other mostly Black, separate, and unequal. I believe that in order to understand the deep sense of helplessness, hopelessness, and malaise that hangs like a cloud over certain parts of our city, you must intentionally spend some time in both Baltimores. You must visit the schools, the corner stores, and the churches. You must catch the buses and walk the streets. You must try to see what it feels like to hang onto the broken pieces and what it feels like when you do not have to do this. This is what I have been doing for the past five months as I have been conducting my unofficial ethnographic study of Baltimore's *hypersegregated* Black neighborhoods. I have been trying to understand what life is like within *The Black Butterfly*, trying to find some answers to the questions that I have been wrestling with since 2015 when a Harvard University study concluded that out of the nation's 100 largest jurisdictions, children born in poverty in Baltimore City have the worst chances of ever escaping it. The study notes that it is even worst for boys because they tend to make roughly 25 percent less income than similar economically challenged boys who were born in other cities. Here in our city, more so than anywhere else in the world, neighborhoods matter. They determine your schools, your health, your well-being, and your future.

As much as possible, I spend my time talking to young people, asking them questions, and trying to listen to them. I want to see the world from their perspective. I want to hear their stories and in some small way, help to shoulder their pain. Part of the reason why I do this is because of Jason, a ninth-grade student from Frederick Douglass High School. I met him in the hallway last year when I hosted a Teach-In at his school. I asked him (like I asked all the students that day) what his plans were for his life and what he wanted to be when he grew up. At first, he did not respond. He turned and leaned up against the locker. He sighed and checked his phone. I just stood there, quiet, hoping that he would answer me. "My father is dead," he said. "My brother is dead. I had two cousins; they got shot. My uncles are locked up. What do I want to be when I grow up? Nothing. I'm from Baltimore; I'm already dead."

I did not say anything. He looked at me and then turned and walked away. I wanted to go after him. I wanted to talk to him and tell him that he was going to be ok. I wanted to ensure him that he could make it, that I was going to help him, and that together we could change his future. I wanted to do and say all of this, but I did not. I felt overwhelmed. Standing in the hallway, it was hard to breathe and hard to imagine a different way forward. His life, according to the data, was being shaped by racially segregated neighborhoods, poverty, poor schools, subpar housing, drugs, gangs, and a history of racism; his response showed that he had been listening, he had been watching, and he is no longer waiting for someone or something to come along and save him. He did not believe that he could be saved and, on that day, standing in the hallway, listening to his story, I failed to tell him that he could. I will not fail again.

Let's fight like hell to save our city

1/23/2020

A few days before the beginning of the new year, I called my father to rant and rave about Baltimore. I was frustrated by the rising homicide numbers and the general air of malaise that had settled over the city and overwhelmed by having to facilitate ongoing conversations on my radio show (Today With Dr. Kaye) about the death and suffering of my people. My father, who is a Southern Baptist minister, quietly listened as I spoke and cried, and then he took me to the book of Esther while weaving in a little bit of Dr. King. "Relief," my father said, "will come to the city of Baltimore, but if you are silent, at this moment, then one day, your silence will be seen as betrayal. And who knows? Perhaps, you were moved to that place for such a time as this. You are in the small space now; hold your ground." I laughed when I hung up because when I was growing up, during the Watch Night, New Year's Eve service my father would always remind the congregation that we had moved into a small space, and we needed to hold our ground. He would tell us, at about 11:55 p.m. (right before the countdown to the New Year), that there is a small space that exists right between who you used to be and who you want to be, where you must stop and make a decision. Do you go forward to carve out a new path, running toward the person you want to be, or do you turn and go back to the familiar path, chasing after who you used to be?

It is in that quiet moment when you are alone, where you must stare into the mirror and take a long loving look at the real you. It is a painful moment, one that might break your soul. It is a place where two roads have diverged, and whichever one you choose, the well-worn or the less traveled, will determine who you are going to be. It is an occasion that must be marked, to record for years to come that something happened, that a decision was made. Marking moments is something that we as human beings do. We mark the moment when a child is born when we get married, or when we fall in love. We record the day when we lose a loved one, when we decide to get sober, and when we realize who we are in this world. We mark these moments because something significant happened. We mark them because they matter. Within small cities, places like Baltimore, we mark our collective shared moments. We look around our beloved city and collectively struggle to reconcile ourselves with the reality that we are both moving forward and standing still. We are in that moment when we must ask ourselves whether we are willing to pay a pound of flesh to save this city. It is very likely that the cost of this battle (to pull us forward into who we want to be) might be more than we are prepared to give. To be clear, it will not be more than what we have; but it might be more than what we are prepared to give.

Baltimore hurts. It takes your breath away and gives you moments when you gasp and clutch your pearls, when you scream and cry out loud, when you go to bed angry and wake up *pissed off.* If you care about the future of this city and if your heart is breaking for what breaks the heart of grieving mothers in this city and if you co-labor with those who are standing at the edge holding back the fire in this city, then your spirit is probably deeply troubled for what has been happening in this city. We are at a moment when if you choose to remain silent about what is happening in this city, then one day, your silence will be seen as a betrayal. This is a moment that will define us for years to come.

As a people, we have been here before. We have come of age in a nation that has been hell-bent on oppressing us, on trying to break us, on attempting to hold us back. We know how it feels to speak up, to pay the pound of flesh, and to move (as Dr. King once said) against all the apathy of conformist thought. We have been here before when the silence of our elected officials spoke volumes and made it clear to us that they care more about themselves than they do about us. We have been here before as a people, and we have been here before as a city. We know what to do. My prayer for Baltimore 2.0 is that this is the year when we reclaim our city, we lean into our city, and we fight like hell to save and transform our city.

Breathing is an act of revolution and rebellion

11/02/2019

As a Black woman and mother in America, every breath that I take is an open act of revolution and rebellion. It is a conscious decision to step into, rather than away from, the light. It requires me to stand and not be moved, to exist in a space between what is possible and what might never be. I make decisions at every turn, trying to live as close as I can to the realm of the possible. I navigate through the grocery store, make my way through the carpool line, and walk confidently across campus, consciously fighting both the White gaze and the imposter syndrome. I am very aware of the "ghost skins," White supremacists who refrain from openly displaying their beliefs to blend into society and further a racist agenda. I know that they are everywhere and live very comfortably at the edges of my reality. There are moments when I must remind myself that I am choosing to be a public intellectual and to openly wrestle with some of the more profound questions around race, identity, and equity that I think we (as a society) need to answer. I am choosing to speak for the unforgotten, to take on the pain, to hear their stories, and to turn them, like a mirror, back onto the world. I want people to be uncomfortable and not be able to sleep at night. The ghost skins get publicly angry at the injustice while privately rooting and fighting for it to continue. Inequity, as they are aware, is one of the bananas that clog the tailpipe of racial justice. These are the same spaces that my great-grandmother would have shied away from.

Growing up, I spent every summer in South Carolina, and I learned, from watching my great-grandmother, how to experience moments of incredible joy within a system that seems hellbent on destroying the tiny pieces that hold you together. She grew up in Olar, South Carolina, a small town with a handful of dusty roads, a plethora of unfulfilled promises, and two of everything else: two schools, one Black, the other White; two churches, one Black, the other White; two doctors, two cemeteries, two corner stores. Even though the town tried to remain legally separated, it was so small that segregation was a conscious and sometimes inconvenient choice. It was a place where people's lives and dreams bumped into one another. In 1963, when my great-grandmother was already into the middle of her life, Dr. King said that the most segregated hour of Christian America was 11 a.m. on Sunday. As a scholar of history, I understood this because I could not imagine that the same White folks who would go out of the way to ignore and degrade Black folks would be able to put that hatred aside to worship and pray together. How do you go from lynching Black bodies to grabbing hands and praying with them and for them? For Black women and mothers, how could they worship with hands stained with the blood of their children? How could Black men and fathers kneel, side by side, with White men who were actively trying to break their spirit?

When I shared Dr. King's words with my great-grandmother (I had just spent a semester studying his work), she vehemently disagreed. She was a small woman, with smooth brown skin, long White hair, and blue eyes. She had cataracts and glaucoma and had been blind as long as I had known her. Whenever we walked, she would place her hand through my arm, and every once in a while, she would tell me to step lightly. Her father was a Tsalagi Indian who had been shot dead by the KKK at their front door for trying to organize the Black community to challenge voter registration. That was the early 1920s, she would explain, when the White man would smile at you when you shopped at his store on Friday, ride through the town and terrorize you on Saturday, and then lead the worship service in his church on Sunday. She said that hour was the most spiritually integrated because, "We were all praying to the same God, and he didn't see color. They thought that he did, but I knew that he didn't. They showed up and smiled in my face and pretended that they spoke for him and that they were concerned for my soul. They didn't speak *for* him; they spoke *to* him, just like I did." She would always raise her voice and lift her chin whenever she talked about the KKK and her father. It was, perhaps, a small act of defiance, a way of not folding herself into the quiet, an act, I would say, of both revolution and rebellion.

Black History Month 2020: you. are. still. here.

2/28/2020

In hindsight, Black History Month probably should have been canceled this year. From the collective grieving over the tragic deaths of Kobe and Gianna Bryant to the misogynistic attack by Snoop Dogg on Gayle King, it has indeed been the worst of times. It is a palpable sense of loss as we collectively grieve the death of someone that we did not personally know, but we feel a deep connection to him and his life. I have read countless tributes and reflections as everyone tried to find a way to express their grief. I cried when #GirlDad trended and immediately picked up the phone to call my father and thank him for the way that he poured his love out to me. I thanked him for being fully present in my life and for being a feminist father long before people even understood what that term meant. I have sat with both grown Black men and young teenagers as they cried over Kobe and felt comfortable sharing their pain and their feelings. When Snoop threatened Gayle, before I could find the words to express my anger, my sons spoke up and stepped into that space to defend

Black women. As my son said to one of his friends, "Even though I don't agree with her questions—it's too soon, in my opinion—I believe that she has the right to ask them without fear of violence from Black men." Yeah, Black Twitter probably should have canceled Black History Month.

When I was growing up, February was always a month of Black joy and Black celebration. It was a time when my father dug out his Kente cloth-laden ministry robes and sprinkled his sermons with the words from some of his favorite Negro Spirituals. It was a month full of singing Black music and learning obscure Black facts. It was the one month out of the year when I believed that White people had to sit with, think about, and bear witness to our contributions to this country. It was a time to help Black people understand that our history is American history, that our story is a part of the larger narrative that describes and defines who we are as a nation. My teachers would line the hallway walls with Black art, the cafeteria would serve soul food, and advertisers would flood the airways with commercials and products and events specifically designed for us.

Even though I was taught that Black history was replete with stories of tragedy and sorrow, in my world, during February, it was just the opposite. It was a moment to take a break from the pain that comes from living and breathing while Black in this country. I grew up in Washington, DC, "Chocolate City," where I lived in a middle-class all-Black neighborhood, attended an all-Black school where some of my teachers either lived on my block or attended my church, and I worshipped at an all-Black church. My life was filled with learning about the history of my people, even when I did not want to hear it. My father would tell us that since the country was going to focus on our pain during Black History Month, he would focus on our joy. Since they planned to focus on our deaths, he would focus on our lives. Since they focused on our tears, then he focused on our laughter. It felt like a month-long house party when we were constantly reminded of how blessed we were to be the descendants of people who chose to survive. Back then, Black History Month was a way of building you up, of lifting your spirit, of providing you with the hope that you needed to get through the rest of the year.

This month has been hard. On that day of the helicopter crash, I was on the phone with both my mother and my son trying to console them. I spent the next day on the radio, listening to my callers share their pain about what happened. Death has a way of reminding us of you and your family's mortality. I found myself checking on my husband and my sons, reaching out and texting just to make sure that they knew that I loved them. I thought a lot about the other parents on the helicopter and the children that they were leaving behind, and I found myself calling my mom every day just to hear her voice. This has been a challenging month, not a happy one or a joyous one, but perhaps a necessary one. Maybe Black History Month is also about taking a moment to stand still and remind yourself that despite everything that has happened, you are still here.

White people hate us because we're Black

3/14/2019

Baltimore feels like a small town, officially divided into nine geographical regions, with over 200 different neighborhoods that are as individual as they are different. I have found that the only way to get a true sense of the lifeblood of this city is to immerse yourself in the different neighborhoods, walk the streets, visit the corner stores, and talk to the people. I would argue that there are two Baltimores, one White and economically advantaged, the other Black and economically challenged—separate and unequal. This system of economic apartheid is like a virus in that it impacts every aspect of a person's life from air quality to life expectancy, from clean drinkable water to lack of dependable regular city services, and from literacy rates to murder rates.

We live in the richest state in the country but within Baltimore City, a predominantly Black city, White residents make almost twice as much as Black residents. Unemployment rates for young Black men are three times higher than those for young White men, and 61% of Black children live in low-income households that have incomes that are less than two times the poverty level. Black Baltimore is struggling. To be clear, life expectancy within

Black neighborhoods, like Upton and Druid Heights, where the median income is about $13,388 a year, is only 63 years, and the residents have a three times higher mortality rate from heart disease, eight times from diabetes, 15 times higher from homicide, and 20 times higher from HIV than in Roland Park, a predominantly White neighborhood, less than five miles away, where the median income is about $90,492 and the life expectancy increases by 20 years. Two Baltimores—separate and unequal.

I hosted a Teen Summit at the Academy for College and Career Exploration, located in Hampden. After visiting so many schools in this city, I was pleasantly surprised at the building. It was clean and bright with a library, tight security protocols, smartboards, microphones, science labs, and computers. I walked through the halls and talked to the students and teachers, and what I found is that although the location and building was new, the students and the problems were not. The school was formerly housed at Lake Clifton Eastern High School, where they struggled with discipline problems, high dropout rates, violence, and low-test scores. According to the teachers, before the school opened in Hampden, the neighborhood rallied and worked to block it. There were community meetings held, and there was a sense that this school, with these students, was not welcome or wanted in this predominantly White community. When I met with the students, they told me that they were routinely called the n-word by White residents who rode by them while they were walking to and from school. Earlier this year, there was a melée between the White residents and the Black students that resulted in the cops being called and a student being arrested. The teachers and the students were adamant that the disturbance was started by the residents and that the students were only defending themselves.

I asked the students to give me a sense of what they believed was happening at their school and in this community. "White people hate us," Peyton, an 11th grader, shouted, "because we're Black and they think we're poor." "Facts," Amir agreed. "They hate us. Every time I go into a White neighborhood, they look at me like I don't belong or that I'm getting ready to wreck some shit up. There are two Baltimores, and we live in the wrong one." One female student jumped in: "Yep, they hate us and it's only because we're Black and that's the one thing that we can't control or change." Ronald stood up and came over and grabbed the mic: "They don't hate us; they're just afraid of us. It's not two Baltimores; it's one city. When the Mayor makes a decision about Baltimore, it affects all of us. When they don't pick up the trash on my block, the whole city is seen as dirty. When somebody gets killed in my hood, people think that all of Baltimore is danger-ous." It was obvious that this was a well-worn topic of discussion because everyone started sharing their stories about their experi-ences with racism and White supremacy and about how they are made to feel like they don't belong in certain parts of Baltimore. Kiwan told me that they talked about it all the time, "We know that there are two Baltimores. We live in one and we go to school in the other. They don't have to tell us we're not welcome; we get it. We know that if they call the police, we're going to jail even if we didn't do or say anything. That's just the way it is." "It's hard sometimes," Peyton said, "because it feels like no matter what we do, they're going to hate us. It's frustrating and I don't know." He looked around at the class for a moment: "Well, we don't know what we can do to change it." "Or," Kiwan said, "if we can change it."

"America," he said, "is a racist wicked hellhole"

5/28/2021

As a Black woman, no matter how fast I run, I cannot outrun my past or our collective history. My life has never been a blank canvas where I could paint the picture of who I want to be and how I want the world to see me. I was born Black in a White world, and I have been fighting to be free, to be equal, to be unbothered in a country that is hellbent on stopping me. "America," my great grandfather, would often say, "is a racist wicked place. A hellhole where, if you are Black, there is no beginning and no end. It just is." As a little girl in Olar, SC, my great-grandfather would take me on long walks through the woods, where we always ended up at the family cemetery no matter what direction we started in. He would walk up and down the rows, stopping to tell me about the person who was buried there. He would weave stories of tragedy and hope, resistance and defiance, incredible will and deep-rooted sadness and remind me that these were the voices that whispered in his ear. These were the roots that kept him tethered to the ground. "Sunya," he would say, using my family nickname, "this is why I can't fly and why I can't leave this place." It takes a lot of courage to be born Black in this country.

Once, when I was in college and visited him, he had bruises all over his face and hands. He did not remember who I was and would often sit and stare out for hours at a time. My Nana said that he was slowly losing his mind. I think that he was trying to fly and leave this place, if only for a moment. Once a week, my great-grandfather would go into town to buy a bag of pecans, and on his last trip, the young White men had jumped him and stolen his money and his bag. The bruises on his face were from where they hit him; the ones on his hands were from where he hit back. I asked him to come with me for a walk. I thought the cemetery would help ground him and bring him back to me, even if it was just for a moment. It was a depressing trip as he walked around in circles, talking so low that I could barely hear him. At one point, he sat down and started pointing at each headstone: White man killed him because he talked too much. They killed him because he was walking too slow. That one there is empty since he never came home; they figured that the White man took him. She died because they hung her son. He was talking and crying. "Last week," he said, "I came by here, and old Mr. Charlie wanted to know what I was doing. I said, 'I'm visiting my family.' He said, 'Boy ain't nothing in that there grave but niggers and ghosts.'" He stopped talking for so long that I thought he was gone again. "Boot," he finally said, "we are more than that. Don't let them make you small. Don't let them break you."

I thought about my great-grandfather this week as I have been wrestling with the racist and painful history of this country and trying hard not to let it break me or make me small. It has been one year since the brutal murder of George Floyd, and this country is still engaged in a battle to change a racist White supremacist system. It has been ugly and challenging and complicated because Mr. Floyd was not the first person, nor has he been the last person to die at the foot of the altar of Whiteness.

The hatred of Black people and the desire not to see us win are rooted in the foundation of this country, and, therefore, they are in the hearts and minds of White people. This is where the battle is and why the terrain is so rough. What does it take to convince White people that Black lives do matter? James Baldwin reminds us that history is not the past; it is the present. We carry our history with us. We are our history.

I thought about Mr. Floyd, and then I thought about Mary Turner, a twenty-one-year-old pregnant Black woman who, after publicly denouncing her husband's lynching, was strung up by her feet, doused with gasoline, and set on fire. Her baby was cut out of her stomach and stomped to death. This happened in 1918, and the same hatred that drove those White men to lynch, burn and shoot her is the same hatred that led Derek Chauvin to keep his knee on the neck of Mr. Floyd for 9 minutes and 29 seconds.

I thought about Mrs. Turner, and then I thought about the Greenwood District in Tulsa, Oklahoma. It was known as Black Wall Street, and it was one of the most prominent concentrations of Black businesses in the country. In 1921, White men, in the space of two days, stalked, tortured, and murdered, hundreds of Black people, tossed their bodies into unmarked graves, and then burned a large portion of the town to the ground. It is a deep-rooted hatred that we are trying to uproot, not outrun. We cannot outrun this nation's past, but we can confront it. We can speak up about it. We can fight against the narrative that our cemeteries are full of niggers and ghosts and not warriors and revolutionaries. We are in a fight to change hearts and minds, to convince this world that Black Lives Matter and that for us to move forward, we must reckon with the past to make sense of the present, and then (and only then) can we prepare for our future.

I swear America will be
America to me

7/31/2021

What will it take, I often wonder, for America—the land of the oppressed, home of racist cowards—to be America to me? What will it take for America—a place where billionaires are playing in outer space while the rest of us are drowning in debt, where people are arguing about vaccines and masks even after almost 700,000 Americans died of COVID—to be a place where I can roam and be free? What will it take for me to love this country enough to believe that it can be better? I think about this often as I come from a long line of people who loved this country. They fought for it, died for it, and believed in it. Our blood is mixed deep within the soil of South Carolina. I come from enslaved people on both sides of my family. On my daddy's side, my ancestors lived on a plantation owned by two brothers, Jim and Dave Draft. I remember hearing these stories when I was younger and realizing early on that our history was entangled with their history. Even before I understood it or could articulate it, I knew that Black history was American history and that American history, when it was taught, included only White history. I knew what it felt like to be erased, which made it hard for me to love this country and call it my own.

My grandfather, my daddy's daddy, loved this country. Even though he grew up in Jim Crow South Carolina and he was called the n-word more times than he could ever admit, he loved the promise of America. It is that America—the one that we talk about, sing about, and pledge our allegiance to—that called to him. It was the dream of that American that kept him moving forward. He would always tell me that we were the heart and soul of this country. "We are survivors," he would say, "and because slavery *couldn't* break us, Jim Crow *didn't*, and White folks *won't*." He used to walk around reciting the Preamble, stopping after every line to add his commentary, and he would tell me that within those 52 words lay the promise of America:

We the people

Sunya, he would say, *it's not Them the People but We and that includes all of us.*

of the United States,

We fought and died for this wretched country to become united, and it is in that bloody union, that we find ourselves.

in order to form a more perfect Union,

A perfect Union can only exist when everyone comes to the table, when we all can contribute our time, our talent, and our treasure to this country.

establish justice,

We want to do more than survive America; we want to thrive in this here nation as well.

insure domestic tranquility,

Words that if actualized could have saved Emmett Till and Dr. King.

provide for the common defense,

We hire the police so that they will protect us, not kill us.

promote the general welfare,

We do this not for ourselves but for you and for the children you may have someday.

and secure the blessings of liberty to ourselves and our posterity,

We fight for freedom and equality. We fight to be left alone and to be free. We fight so that our shoulders are strong enough for the next generation to stand on.

do ordain and establish this Constitution for the United States of America.

This is why I love this country; no matter what they do or what they try to tell us, this is our land. We built this country, and nobody can take that from us.

"There's never been equality for me," Hughes goes on to write, "nor freedom in this 'homeland of the free.'" Only we, my grandfather, would sigh and say, can make America America. He was one of the first people who taught me about fighting for justice within an unjust society. He taught me about equality and equity even though he had never experienced either of them. He taught me how to hold my head up, face racism and racists without flinching or tearing up or breaking a sweat. It is during those moments when I feel that I am in a fight to save this country that I think about my grandfather and his life. He was a gentleman, a deacon, and a farmer. He used to rest his hand on my head when I was a little girl. He smelled like freedom, and I swore that I could see the whole world in his eyes. He spoke quietly but firmly. He stuttered just a little and would make a point to repeat his most salient points. He wanted to make sure that we understood him. When I was getting ready to go to college, I called him for some advice. I wanted him to be proud of me. When I told him that I was getting ready to leave, I could hear the smile and the pride in his voice. "Go now and change the world," he started laughing, "because you can. Don't let those White folks stop you or try to contain you. They don't hold your freedom in their hands. When you were a baby, I used to whisper in your ears. I told you all the dreams I had for you. Those words are inside of you; they will come back to your remembrance when you need them the most. This is our country, now go and reshape it with your hands." I wrote those words down, and every time I feel like the weight of this ol' racist nation is threatening to bring me down, I pull them out, read them out loud to remind me of who I am and what America could be for me.

I come from a long line of angry Black women

6/12/2020

My grandmothers were brave, strong, courageous, and able to withstand great force and pressure. They were Black women in America, and they learned how to turn their anger into activism and their strength into survival. I come from a long line of strong and angry Black women. My Nana used to say that you have to decide whether you are willing to die for your freedom in this country. She said that this was a daily decision that Black women had to confront and settle. She was angry all the time, and she said that being a Black mother in this country meant that you had to be prepared to fight every day: for your life and for the life of your children. You had to be willing to stand between the world and your children. You had to be ready to die so that they could live free. Black women are the consciousness—the awareness and the sentience—of this racist and soul-sick society. We were there when they stole us from our home, and we watched as some of our people chose to jump overboard rather than journey to an unknown land. We were angry then, but we chose to survive. We know that the route to the Americas is riddled and lined with our bones. We were there when they inspected us, bargained over us, raped us, and stole our children from us. We were angry then, but we chose to survive.

One of those women born in slavery was my great-grand-mother's grandmother. I am only six generations from being enslaved. She was born at the tail end of the Civil War, and though she did not grow up enslaved, she carried the memories and the stories with her. She would speak her truth, my Nana would say, to anyone who could shoulder the weight of the pain. She was a big woman: bold, Black, and brilliant. She refused to be broken or terrified into submission. She survived slavery, and as a little girl in Olar, South Carolina, she witnessed the birth of the Ku Klux Klan. Founded only six days after the ratification of the 13th Amendment, the KKK was one of many secret White societies founded to restore White order and rule back to the South. She remembered the Klan riding through the town, and it made her angry. She believed that the greatest weapon that Black mothers had was our ability to survive the Whiteness of this world so that our children could one day defeat it. Black women, she said, knew how to survive and how to fight.

We have been fighting against this system since we arrived here. In 1654, some three hundred and twelve years before the beginning of the modern civil rights era, the first documented Black protest happened in America. Eleven enslaved men and women from New Netherland (later renamed New York) petitioned and won both their freedom and their land. The earliest account of a planned slave rebellion (it was discovered before it happened), occurred in 1687 on a plantation in Virginia. My great grandmother was six months old when the KKK showed up at the door of her home and shot and killed her father. He was both West Indian and a member of the Navajo tribe and had been working to organize the Black vote. She grew up watching her mother struggling to survive in the same town around the men who killed her husband. She remembered how her mother picked up her father's work and continued to try to get Black people to have the courage to exercise their right to vote. She was a warrior, and she operated with a degree of alertness, alacrity, diligence, and anger. She had one standing rule that had been passed down by every Black woman in my family: we protect the children. We put them behind us. We shield them, we love them, and we nurture them. We survive Whiteness so that they can one day defeat it.

My mother called me after she saw the video of George Floyd, and she said that when he called for his mother, every muscle and bone and tendon in her body reacted. She said that he was not just calling for his mother; he was calling for all Black mothers. His cry was one that stretched back to the first child stolen from Africa who called for their mother as they were being led onto that ship. It was the same cry that a child made when they were being sold from their mother and shipped from Jamestown to Columbia. It was the same cry that Emmett Till or Tamir Rice or Trayvon Martin probably made in those last final moments. Black mothers, she said, were ignited that day once again, and now we must heed the call. We must get angry, and then we must fight.

An open call to Black mothers

6/6/2019

As painful as it is to admit, there is a dark cloud that hangs over our city. It is thick with our pain and made heavy by our tears. It is a very subtle reminder that maybe some burdens are so heavy, we cannot carry them alone. It is hard being a Black mother in America and harder still being a Black mother in Baltimore City. I have come to the realization that not everyone is built to withstand the emotional price that Black mothers must pay in this city. We must shoulder incredible pain while helping our children have moments of unspeakable joy. From the first day we drop our children off in a school that is not welcoming or bright or beautiful, we immediately learn how to swallow our pain, throw our back against the wind, and do what we can to make it through. We have both an unrelenting fierceness and an unshakable sense of foreboding. We understand more than anyone else that this city does not love or value or even appreciate our children. We know that no one is coming to save our children and that we must do all we can to hold them up, to lift them higher, to help them to see the genius of who they are. For some of us, our goal is to get our children home safely every night; for others, we just want to get them out of this city to a place of safety and refuge.

As a researcher and a mom, I spend my days going through this city, visiting schools, talking to people, and trying to get a sense of what makes Baltimore tick. I want to know who we are and who we hope to become. I want to be able to speak our truth, articulate our pain, and then make some sense out of it. I want to be able to take this truth and tell it to my sons. Baltimore City teaches you how to have grit and testicular fortitude. It forces you to be resilient, to have intrinsic motivation, and to be able to see beyond this narrative to what you want to be on the other side. I want to write it across their heart. I want them to go places I have never been and engage in conversations that I will never have. I want them to be happy and healthy and whole. I want so much for them, but as a Black mother in Baltimore City what I want more than anything else is for them to survive, to live, to see another day.

I thought about this last week as Baltimore City commemorated the 2nd Annual City Schools Peace and Remembrance Day. It was a day to remember the children who did not live to get to the end of the school year. Seniors who will never graduate and seventh graders who will never go to high school. We stopped to remember the first grader who will never learn to color or the junior who will never attend prom. We stopped to stand still for just a moment to weep for what we have lost. It was a moment that was painful and hard. It was a moment that calls on us to do more because this city is dangerous, and right now, it is out of control.

Last year, nine names were read; this year, Dr. Sonja Santelises, the CEO of Baltimore City School, read 12 names, and after each name, a bell was rung. Twelve names. Twelve bells. Twelve children who lost their life due to senseless gun violence. Nikki Giovanni once said we must invent the future through our blood and tears, through all this sadness. Here in Baltimore City, as Black mothers, we are now being called to do just that. We must take our pain and turn it into a future promise for our children. We must take our mourning and turn it into a movement. We must partner with Mothers of Murdered Sons and Daughters, Inc., the Baltimore Ceasefire, and the Baltimore Algebra Project, to name just a few, and help them to do the hard work. Sisters, as painful as this may sound, no one is coming to save us. We must save ourselves because these are our children. We love them. We see them. And now we must lean in and protect them.

Let this roll call of Baltimore City school children who died be the last one that is ever read in this city: Taylor Hayes, 7; Montrell Mouzon, 14; Markell Hendricks, 16; Cameron Anderson, 17; Mekhi Anderson, 17; Lamont Green, 17; Michael Handy, 17; Corey Moseley, 17; Des'Mon Anderson, 18; Marcus Brown, 18; Damian Claridy, 18; Markise Jackson, 19.

Black history is American history

2/26/2019

Growing up in Washington, DC, in a small all-Black community full of teachers and pastors and government workers, I learned early on that Black history is American history. There were days when my father and his friends would interrupt our game of Freeze Tag or Simon Says to teach us about our history. We were told, more than once, that our history did not begin and end with slavery. Africans arrived in this country and worked as indentured servants, just like everyone else. We were taught that the Christopher Columbus 1492 Arrival story was a lie and that as Black people, we were a part of the 1619 legacy. It was not until I was a college student, majoring in history, that I finally began to make the connections between 1619 and the beginning of the Black American history story.

It was in late August 1619, at Point Comfort on the James River, that the first 20 Africans arrived on the shores of this country aboard the White Lion, an English ship. They were sold in exchange for food and later transported to Jamestown, where they were placed on indentured servant contracts. Given that Virginia's General Assembly had not yet worked out the terms for what constituted enslavement in the colony, it is likely that they received the same rights, duties, privileges, responsibilities, and punishments as White indentured servants. Five years later, in 1624, two of the people from that ship, Anthony and Isabella, had a son, William Tucker, who was the first person of African ancestry born in the 13 British Colonies. Although very little is known about his life, records suggest that he was born at Fort Monroe, baptized in Jamestown, and named after Captain William Tucker, who held his parents' indentured contracts.

When I first read through the research, I was reminded of what my father used to always tell us: Black History is American History. It has been 400 years since Black people arrived in this country and we are at a moment when we must pause to reflect on what it means to be the descendants of people who survived being born Black in this country. We have survived four hundred years of constant brutal attacks on our Blackness. We have endured four hundred years of degradation, humiliation, pain, death, and fear. And, yet we are still here. They did not break us. They did not stop us. They did not erase us. They did not kill our joy, our faith, and our absolute belief in justice. We survived, and it is not because of magic; it is because we come from people who chose every single day to survive.

We are here at a moment that will define us, where we must decide who we want to be, what we want to be remembered for, and how we want to contribute to this current movement for humanity. We are witnessing a moment, during a week of what would have been Trayvon Martin's 24th birthday, that Black Lives Matter is actively being taught in the classroom while Virginia Governor Ralph Northam defends his use of wearing Blackface. It is a week when Stacey Abrams became the first Black woman to give a Democratic rebuttal to our nation's first Whitelash president. It is a moment when we are dealing with the reality that across the country unarmed Black people are still being shot by the police while right here in Baltimore, our homicide numbers within *The Black Butterfly* neighbors are slowly inching up.

Frederick Douglass once said that Black people watered the soil of America with their tears, nourished it with their blood, and tilled it with their hands. As a Black woman, it makes me proud to realize and understand that we helped to build this country and that we are one of the reasons why it is so great. Ninety-three years ago, Carter G. Woodson launched Negro History Week, as a time to remember and teach about Black history. In 1976, it was expanded to a month and became an internationally recognized time of celebration. I grew up celebrating Black History Month in February and being taught Black history from March to January. As both a supporter and a critic of Black History Month, I hold fast to the hope that one day we will not need a designated month to remind people of who we are, but that people will recognize that Black History is American History. And as such, it should be regularly taught in the schools, around the dinner tables, on long drives across the country, and in the middle of Fortnight games and Netflix challenges. This is how we rise, how we move forward, and how we honor those who decided to survive so that we could thrive.

A city at war

10/3/2018

Reading about Baltimore City through the lens of a Black mother offers the outside world an analytical framework for trying to interpret and understand the intricacies of what it is like to move through a city that is currently at war. This is not a war in the traditional sense of the word, as bombs are not dropping from the sky and napalm is not being released into the air, but it is a war, being played out in real-time, between the way things are at this moment and the way things ought to be. Baltimore City is a violent place. With 39 homicides within the last 30 days and 234 homicides (as of October 2) this year, it is a city that is at war with itself. It is not comfortable. It is not safe. And it is not normal. We are besieged with disturbing images and stories of community violence and predatory policing which are coupled with the reality of our run-down neighborhoods, our food deserts, and our crumbling schools. This can only be seen as a set of social scripts that are, as Patricia Collins writes, the legacy of racism, sexism, class exploitation...that assign categories of superiority and inferiority. In this sense, a Black mother's words and pain can then act as the critical social theory that is needed to explain how Black people, living within what Lawrence Brown calls a Category Five hyper-segregated apartheid city, are marginalized, and oppressed through institutional structures and practices, social norms, and ideological elitism. It also can help to explain the violence and the rage.

James Baldwin once wrote that to be a Negro in this country and to be relatively conscious is to be in a rage almost all the time. Rage leads to violence, and it cannot be hidden though it can be dissembled and dissimulated. There are no simple solutions to ending the violence or the rage. Additionally, once you add race and you look at the work of psychiatrists William H. Grier and Price M. Cobbs, you realize that "Black rage," which stems from the desperation, the conflict, and the anger that comes from being Black in America, is what is being played out across this city. Black rage is what it feels like to live in a city where your children attend schools with leaky roofs, busted pipes, and faulty sprinkler systems. It is what it feels like when there are no recreation centers or green spaces for young people to go to when the school day ends. It is what it feels like when politicians, once elected, spend their days talking about the problems without ever offering viable and workable solutions. Black rage is what it feels like to live in a city that gives tax breaks to millionaire businessmen while failing to raise the minimum wage for the working poor. It is what it feels like to work hard every day and never be able to work yourself out of poverty. It is what it feels like to watch a generation of young Black men shoot and kill each other without any regard for their lives or for their communities or for their futures. Black rage is what it feels like when your children are unable to drink the water in their school and you are unable to receive free services to help treat the lead that is already in their bodies. It is what it feels like to be in a war and what it feels like to live in Baltimore.

I have spent years trying to figure out how to navigate through my Black rage and how to operate within a city that is not designed for me to be free or to get free. It is complicated. It is messy and it is hard. This wave of violence, that is sweeping through our city, feels like a cancer that is feeding off our terror and our pain. We find ourselves at a moment when we do not need more statistics or sociological studies, conference papers or empty promises because no child deserves to grow up in a city where the hardest part of the day is just getting through the streets safely. They deserve to be safe. If we cannot find a way to end this war for ourselves, as adults who should know how to solve difficult problems, then we must find a way to do it for them. Our children deserve to demand and expect more from us. They deserve to hold us to the highest standards, to expect us to do right by them, to hold us accountable for helping to maintain a system that is designed to fail them and is unable to protect them. They deserve for us not to just try but to solve the impossible. We are at war and our terror dome is filled with the loud sounds of gunshots and the silent screams of our children, and we can no longer believe or pretend that just because we do not hear or we do not want to, then they do not exist.

We will march on 'til victory is won

8/31/2019

The reality that after four hundred years, we still must prove to both the world and to some within our community that our lives, Black lives, matter, is both a toxic reality and a painful realization. It is a burden that is made more onerous by the years of injustice, the tears shed, and the protests mounted. In August 1619 when the first 20 Africans landed here in English North America, they did so, not knowing what the future held for them or whether they were going to survive and thrive in this new world. They arrived on a cloudy day, aboard the "White Lion," a Dutch man-of-war ship that was carrying enslaved cargo from the Kingdom of Ndongo in Angola. That the information was recorded is astonishing; that it has survived is a miracle because it provides us with a small window that opens up our history on these native shores. Among the "20 and odd Negroes" were Antoney and Isabell, a couple who would later marry and give birth to William, the first documented African baby baptized in this new world. They were survivors who chose to go forward rather than backward. Their story, which is piecemealed together by fading documents and a vibrant oral history, paints a picture that shows that they were captured, enslaved, and later freed all while building their family and amassing a small fortune. For so many of us, who cannot trace and document the beginning of our lives in this country, Antoney and Isabell are a beacon of hope, an example of what it looks like to choose to survive in this country.

It has been four hundred years, and we have survived. Four hundred years of Black resilience and Black joy, of Black family and Black love. Four hundred years of White nationalism and White supremacy of racism and oppression. Four hundred years of experiencing both war and peace in this country. We have survived and we must use this as a moment of awakening where we must remember that power, as Frederick Douglas taught us, never concedes without a struggle. This survival instinct must be a rallying cry that makes its way into every community. We are at a middle passage moment when we must recognize that we have survived seeing Black bodies lynched and terrorized, choked and beaten, shot and killed and despite this very painful reality, we are choosing (once again) to go forward rather than backward.

This is a moment where we must remember that despite our best intentions and our work to make this country a more perfect union, there are still some spaces in this country where our lives do not matter, but this is not new. Our collective memory reminds us that we have been at this moment before. We were at this moment in the colonies when slavery was legalized, and Black folks were enslaved from the womb to the grave. We were at this moment during Reconstruction when the rise of White domestic terrorism began to slow the wave of Black progress and change. We were at this moment when they murdered Emmett Till, when they shot Medgar Evers and Malcolm X and Martin Luther King Jr., and, when they blew up the 16th Street Baptist Church. We were at this moment when they bombed MOVE and burned down Black Wall Street and Rosewood. We have been at this moment before. We know that it is time to mobilize and plan, come together, and strategize. It is time to remember and then go forward. It is time to reclaim our neighborhoods, reclaim our children, and reclaim the future that we have worked for four hundred years to have in this country. We must mark this occasion and celebrate our strength and build up our faith

If Earth is a woman, then America is a man

9/9/2021

Arundhati Roy once wrote that "Another world is not only possible, but she is also on her way. On a quiet day, I can hear her breathing." I would add that in these moments, as we watch what is happening in Texas with Senate Bill 8 and Senate Bill 4, we must remember to listen for her breath. We must not forget to be calm in the middle of the storm, unless we are the storm, and then we must destroy whatever is in the path that seeks to contain us and make us small. We must take their hands and their laws out of our wombs. We must remind them again that our bodies, even though they have long been seen as a space for the taking, for laws, political discussion, and religious debate, belong only to us. I say this as a Black feminist who understands that my visible and unseen intersectional scars are a road map telling the story of a country whose pursuit of manifest destiny cuts straight to the core of who I am. I also grew up in the church, and I was taught, as far back as I can remember, that I am a descendant of Eve, and, if you let men tell the story, I am defiant. I am wicked. I am headstrong and stubborn. I am cursed, and therefore must be controlled for my own good. "White men, all men," my *Black*

Feminist Theory professor once said, "must be stopped before they blow up the planet or take us into another war." They must be stopped, I added, before they rip out our wombs (again) and lay them on the table as chits for the taking.

If Earth is a woman, then America, with all its hatred, destruction, murder, inequities, and violence, is a man. In 1776, Thomas Jefferson wrote that all *men* are created equal. In Section 2 of the Fourteen Amendment, gender was introduced into the US Constitution and being a man meant that you had protected rights. Two years later, when the Fifteenth Amendment was ratified prohibiting the federal government and each state from denying a citizen the right to vote based on that citizen's "race, color, or previous condition of servitude." It said *citizen*, but it meant *men*.

In 1888, when Frederick Douglass argued that no man can either speak, vote, act or be responsible for a woman, he was one of only a handful of men who spoke out against the universality of man's rule over woman. He said that since men had always ruled over women, they had come to believe that ruling over women was their right. It took decades of organizing and protesting before women could vote, attend school, own property, get credit cards and have body autonomy. Just like Black people had to fight to be free because of the color of our skin, women had to fight to be free because of our wombs. Today, women make up over 51% of the population, are the most educated, and hold positions from vice president of the United States to college presidents. Yet, Texas has reminded us that our bodies are not our own, and when we become pregnant, either by choice or through tragic circumstances, we lose body autonomy. Pregnancy is the knife that cuts off our tongue. But this type of control, this universality of rule over a woman's body, has always been part of the fabric of this country. Early on, American colonies followed the laws and ways of their mother countries and women and girls were vessels belonging to their father before becoming a *femme covert*, with no legal existence apart from their husbands.

One of the historical throughlines of this country is the work that men have done to control our bodies and cut out our tongues. This is what is happening in Texas with Senate Bill 8 (SB8) and Senate Bill 4 (SB4). SB8 bans abortions after the sixth week of pregnancy (which for many women is the moment when they realize that they are pregnant); allows anyone to bring a lawsuit against medical practitioners who violate the ban; and provides cash bounties of at least $10,000 (plus legal fees and costs) to encourage any private citizen to sue anyone who is suspected of aiding, abetting, or having an abortion after week six. SB4 prohibits physicians from prescribing drugs that contain levonorgestrel, the effective ingredient in what is commonly referred to as the "morning-after pill," to women who are more than seven weeks pregnant.

What is deeply concerning in this is the failure of the Supreme Court to prevent SB8 from being enacted (which is yet another reminder of why elections matter). At this moment, we have a very conservative majority ruling the Supreme Court and interpreting laws and setting precedents that can shape this country for the next 100 years. (And before you argue that I am overstating the importance of the long arm of this moment, remember that *Plessey v. Ferguson*, the case that legalized segregation, was decided in 1896, and the case that overturned it, *Brown v. Board of Education*, was decided in 1954. Sixty-nine years later, we are still dealing with racial discrimination, school inequity, and the fight to convince White America that Black lives matter.) The battle over my womb is as contentious and as deep-rooted as the battle over my skin. Both belong to me but are being argued and debated, litigated, and discussed by bodies and faces that are not like mine. "White skin and penises," my professor once said, "are the *radix causa* of every one of my nightmares, and until I get their hands off my body and out of my womb, I will never be free. I will never be safe. And I will never be able to rest." I am assuming that like thousands of women across the country and me, she has not slept well since Texas rolled out the blueprint that will be used by other states to gut or overturn the protections that *Roe v. Wade* provide. The road to freedom, to dismantle this legal *salus in arduis*, once again, goes through my womb.

Juneteenth: celebrating through our tears

6/16/2022

On Jan. 1, 1863, Emilie Frances Davis, a 21-year-old freeborn Black woman, sat in her room in Philadelphia, PA, pulled out her pocket diary, wrote her name in ink and cursive on the first page, and proceeded to describe her day. The day was historic: it was Jubilee Day, the moment when the "throat of slavery" intersected with the "keen knife of liberty" as the nation, with the release of the Emancipation Proclamation, began a slow march toward liberty and justice for all. It was also a day of marked contradictions because the Confederate states that had seceded from the Union were unwilling to concede.

One hundred days before the final document was released, President Abraham Lincoln, while speaking in Antietam, MD, signed a preliminary Emancipation Proclamation—offering the Confederate states a final opportunity to either rejoin the Union or risk the immediate emancipation of their "slaves." It was not intended to be a pro-Black benevolent document; it was a war tactic, a political statement. For the Black community, the potential release of this Proclamation was the first step in that slow march. As Jacqueline Jones explains it, emancipation "was not a gift bestowed upon passive slaves by Union soldiers or presidential proclamation; rather, it was a process by which Black people ceased to labor for their masters and sought instead to provide directly for one another."

As it is today, during that time, America was deeply divided. It was at war, and even though Lincoln and other White male power brokers said the war was nothing more than a "simple misunderstanding between gentlemen, a White man's War," the real issue was the continuation and expansion of the peculiar and evil institution called slavery. It was a billion-dollar industry that had continued unchecked for over 240 years. By 1860, most millionaires in this country were Southern slaveholders, and the economic value of four million enslaved people was about $3.5 billion. Slavery was a brutal system. Frederick Douglass, in his speech, "What to the Slave is the Fourth of July," argued that slavery was designed to turn Black men into brutes by robbing them of their liberty, working them without wages, keeping them ignorant, beating them with sticks, raping the boys and girls, flaying their flesh, loading their limbs with iron, hunting them with dogs when they dared to try to claim their freedom, knocking out their teeth, selling them at auctions, and starving them into obedience and submission.

This type of brutality, I would say, does not turn Black men into brutes but reveals the brute in the White men who see this as just behavior. As Matthew Desmond explains, to understand the brutality of American capitalism, you have to start on the plantation. In the same vein, if you want to understand why the notions of freedom are so hard to explain, you have to start with the lies rooted in the celebration of the Proclamation. Lincoln's goal was not to end slavery but to save the Union. Slavery was not supposed to end, and when it did, we were not supposed to survive. So, on that day, when the news of "emancipation" swept across the nation, the night of celebration was electric. Colonel Thomas Wentworth Higginson, a White abolitionist from the First South Carolina Volunteer Regiment, later noted that the tribute to the news of Jubilee sounded like "the choked voice of a race at last unloosed."

Douglass, who spoke at the Tremont Church moments after the Proclamation was released, said, "Remembering those in bounds as bound with them, we wanted to join in the shout for freedom, and in the anthem of the redeemed." But the news of freedom, like freedom itself, moved slowly.

Union soldiers were tasked with taking the word from plantation to plantation, so it was not until June 19, 1865, that the 250,000 enslaved people in Texas (the outermost part of the Confederate States of America) received the news that they had been emancipated. One year later, they held the first Juneteenth celebration to mark their moment of freedom. Even though the Emancipation Proclamation did not legally end slavery (that did not happen until Dec. 6, 1865, with the ratification of the 13th Amendment), Black people have used that moment and every moment since then to make America live up to its creed to be both the home of the brave and the home of the free. Even though true freedom has yet to arrive, we recognize Juneteenth as a day of celebration, education, and agitation. We mark this occasion with tears and with joy because we understand that we were not supposed to survive, but we did.

For a Black mother, freedom is a whole word

9/21/2021

As a Black mother, it is not enough to dream of a world where your children are safe and where they can be free. It is not enough to trust that the system will police itself or believe that without rigorous oversight, police officers or politicians or teachers will look at your Black son or daughter and assume the best and not conclude the worse. Black mothering is a long act of courage. I cannot be the only Black woman who cried when I realized that I was bringing a man-child into this world. I know that I am not the only Black mother who spent hours while my sons were growing up, trying to think of how I could keep them safe. I worried while they were in elementary school, attending a private school where my oldest was the only African American boy in his grade, and my youngest was one of four. I listened carefully as they described their day, their interactions with their teachers and other students. I listened with a Black mother's ear for the subtle moments of racial microaggressions that happened when they were overlooked or when they were singled out. I spent more days at that school and more nights than I can remember standing at their door, praying over them, watching over them, and sometimes crying over them. I worried while they were in middle school, where my oldest was now one of two, and my youngest, who had moved to an inner-city, predominantly Black school, was now struggling with trying to fit into a world that was new to him. I listened with a Black mother's ear as my youngest described daily bathroom fights, confrontations in the hallway and standing still while a Black teacher threatened to slap him with all that she had in her. I started every day with a meeting with the principal as I worked to find him a new school.

I worried more while they were in high school because they were bigger and older and because, as young Black men, they were seen as threats. Even though we are in Baltimore, White supremacy is a *rhizomorph*, a Black shoestring filament buried so deep within the American soil that it is tied to the roots of this country. It is a dark beast that exists even within the brightest spaces. It is why we march, why we protest and why Black mothers are the bridges that carry our children over. I worked. I watched. And I worried. I wanted to get them through school and get them to college. I know that that is not the end, but it is a different beginning. When my father dropped me off at college, he gave me an empty box and told me that it was full of their (my parents') prayers and tears, hopes and dreams. He said that whenever I had a problem believing in myself or whenever I did not think I was going to make it, I should look at the box and remember that I am living the life that my grandparents wanted me to have, the life that they wished they could have had. Two years ago, my husband and I "gave" that box to our oldest son, and two weeks ago, we gave it to our youngest. They are the best of what we have to offer the world, and they are the hope and the dreams of our enslaved ancestors.

Before I left him on campus, my son asked me to leave him with a word, something that he could chew on and that would make him think. He wanted a word that could also be a goal. I gave him *freedom* because *freedom is* a whole word. It is a word rooted in action, a word rooted in love, and as I so often told my sons, it is a word rooted in both sacrifice and death. For freedom to live, oppression must die, and White supremacy must be in a body bag right next to it. For freedom to survive and grow, we must plant commitment and sacrifice right beside it. I grew up having conversations with my father about freedom and what it meant to demand it, not ask for it. I used to hear him arguing with his friends about what freedom meant and whether they had what it would take to make freedom real. "Are you willing to die so that others can be free," he would say, "because if you are in this only so that you can be free, then it will never happen." Freedom, as Malcolm X once said, ain't free. And freedom, according to Coretta Scott King, is never really won; you earn it and win it in every generation. And freedom, as Dr. King reminded us, is never given voluntarily by the oppressor; it must be demanded by the oppressed. I left him with freedom, like how Mary McLeod Bethune left us with love and hope and a thirst for education. My job was to leave him with freedom, and his job over the next four years is to figure out how to get it. Audre Lorde once wrote that it is your dreams that point the way to freedom. I believe that my ancestors dreamed of freedom, of equal access, and of providing a path so that their children could become the best of who they are. Those dreams long planted began to germinate when my father went to college; they began to sprout when I went, and now, through my sons, those dreams are starting to bloom and blossom.

Black History Month 2023: the power of Black resistance

2/1/2023

In 1644, as our nation was still in the very early stages of growth and development, the first documented moment of Black protest and resistance happened in America. Eleven enslaved men and women living in the Black community of New Amsterdam, the principal port city and capital, petitioned for and won their freedom and land. They had completed seventeen of their eighteen years of indentured servitude. They argued that they should be freed and not subject to the 1625 Virginia law that was beginning to be adopted in the colonies. This law distinguished between Black servitude and Black slavery and laid the groundwork for the harsher, more substantial slave laws that took effect beginning in 1657. Although that was the first documented racial protest, it was probably not the first one to happen and definitely not the last. The earliest account of a rebellion by enslaved men and women occurred in 1687 on a plantation in Virginia. Even though their plan was discovered before it happened, the idea that Black people were organizing back then to aggressively challenge the system is important to note.

There has always been multiple movements and ideas within the Black community around resistance. This means that there was protest happening in the streets and in the courtroom, and that there were some Black folks working for our community and working against our best collective interest. The understanding of all of these realities helps to frame the Black American experience. The struggle and desire to be free, to write our history, and to pursue our destiny have long been a part of that experience, and despite laws designed to restrict rights and freedoms, it has remained a central part of the story. The questions have never been about whether we should get involved in the struggle for civil rights, but rather when, where, and to what extent.

As America has continued to advance—from its early days as a young nation to its current role as a world power—Black people have both contributed to but have not always benefitted from the collective advancement. These struggles and protests did not just involve fighting for land and physical freedom; they also extended to fighting for the promises embedded within our foundational documents. Many of these questions, asked since the beginning of this American experiment, are still being asked today. On the surface, using a 21st-century lens, the questions about liberty and justice for all are simple but when one uses the long eye of history, these questions cut to the heart of who we are and who is a part of the American story. Black history is American history, and it is a truth that we are trying to hold within a system built on whiteness and sustained by white supremacy. We hold these truths to be self-evident and have been willing to fight and die for them. "How can you," my father once asked, "face the truth of America and not be so angry that you want to burn it all down?" My mother would sigh and add, "How do you burn down the house you live in?" This is the American experience, for many Black people—trying to burn down a house and save it at the same time.

This tension has led to frequent movements for civil rights: it happened in the courtroom in 1849, with the *Roberts v. City of Boston* case, as lawyers unsuccessfully argued that legalized segregation psychologically damaged black students, and on the streetcars in 1867 when Caroline Le Count, a freeborn educated woman, engaged in civil disobedience to force the city to enforce the law that integrated public transportation. It happened in 1851 when Sojourner Truth, at the Akron Convention, challenged a committee of men to think about the rights of women and again one year later when Frederick Douglass challenged Americans to think about the significance of the *Fourth of July* in the lives and experiences of African Americans. The early movement for civil rights, from the cotton fields in the South to the cotton shirts in the North, was extremely active and provided the roots upon which the modern Civil Rights Movement was built. We have learned since then that the battle for civil rights is not just about changing laws, practices, policies, and procedures, but it is about changing the hearts and minds of racist White folks and complicit Black folks. We are not just fighting those outside of our community but those within our communities as well.

The Black History Month Theme for 2023 was Black Resistance, which is an essential part of who we are and a necessary tool that helps us to reconcile what it means to both live in the house and burn it down. Black people, I was always taught, are the heart and soul of this nation. We are the canaries in the minefield who cry out when this nation strays too far from who it is supposed to be for all of us. We believe in the idea of the American dream, just not the reality. We too sing America; we just want to do it with our own voices and with our own song.

~~five minutes before the~~
~~Klan shows up~~
my father's yesterday

The best time to plant a tree
was fifty years ago.
The second-best time is right now.
And if you are not planting at this moment,
you are already too late.

Nigger is not my name

3/27/2019

I grew up learning how to hold my rage, to swallow my pain, and to stand up tall even when I felt like I had the weight of the world on my shoulders. I spent every summer in South Carolina around women who had come of age during the days of Jim Crow and who made it a point to teach me about the power and strength of Blackness. There were days when it was overwhelming (exhausting, really) to be Black and to have to deal with Whiteness as the standard through which everything else was measured. My grandmother despised this standard and the notions of White privilege. Her neighborhood was filled with Confederate flags and White men who dared to call her auntie. She remembers being called nigger almost as much as she was called by her name. I was seven the first time that I can remember being called a nigger. My grandmother used that moment to teach me how to respond and say, with confidence and without bending my head, that nigger was not my name. She made me stand in front of the mirror and say it over and over again until I could say it without tears in my eyes, without looking away, and without internalizing the power of this word. She told me that some words were designed to strip Black people of both our power and our voice. "White people," she said, "need us to be their niggers so that they can feel superior. Don't give them that. Nigger is not your name, nor your legacy. You may not understand that today, but you will, and when you do, make sure you tell somebody else."

I thought about my grandmother's words while I was preparing to speak at the Maryland Lynching Memorial Project. I sat in my office watching videos and looking through photographs of Black bodies hanging from trees. I studied the faces of the White men and women who were casually standing around, talking, and laughing, as Black people were being tortured and abused, cut, and burned. I looked at the children and wondered who they grew up to be, after learning to normalize Black death and suffering. I listened to interviews from White people who spoke about why they had to kill that nigger, almost as if they were doing God's work. The nigger to them was a nameless and faceless monster that threatened White supremacy, White nationalism, and White superiority. The nigger, as James Baldwin once said, is an invention of White people that show their fear of Black people.

According to the Equal Justice Initiative, nearly 3,959 Black men, women, and children were lynched in the twelve Southern states between 1877 and 1950, and so far, 40 of them have been documented to have happened right here in Maryland. On that day, I wanted to speak their names and to speak for the victims that had not been identified yet. I wanted to say, loud and clear, that nigger was not their name. I wanted to speak for those who had been terrorized, those who had been stalked, those who had been harassed, and those who had been beaten and tortured. I wanted to speak for them because those who are still here must not forget. We must hold the power of collective memory and teach it to others. I thought about all of this when I visited Bard High School Early College in Baltimore. I walked into the school and walked past a group of Black male students laughing and calling each the n-word. I was on my way to the office, but I decided to stop and ask them why they were using that word. Now, that was not the first time that I heard young people use the n-word, but after spending so many days immersed in lynching history, I could not just walk by. They said that it was a form of affection and that it was not a big deal. They said that everybody did it and that it was ok if you were Black.

I stood there and looked at them because I wanted to tell them about the history of this word and about what James Baldwin said. I wanted to show them the lynching pictures on my phone and talk about how our blood, as Frederick Douglass once said, is mixed with the soil of this land. I wanted to challenge them to think deeply about the power of their words, but I did not know where to start. How do you collapse 400 hundred years of oppression and hatred of White supremacy and White nationalism, lynching, and torture into five minutes? As I stood there thinking about all of this, the hallways filled up, and the students started moving toward class. One young man stayed behind because he wanted to know why I questioned them and what was the big deal with that word. I thought about my grandmother at that moment, and I smiled, because nigger, I said, is not your name nor your legacy. You may not understand that today, but you will, and when you do, make sure you tell somebody else.

Fighting through the White gaze

10/12/2017

On any given day, I find myself wrestling with two realities: what it means to be Black and what it means to be Black in Baltimore City. I struggle to see myself through a long lens that does not rely solely upon the White gaze. I look through the threads of history searching for moments that reveal our creativity, our tenacity, and our plain outright stubbornness. I must remind myself that we are survivors, having survived American enslavement, Jim Crow, Reaganomics, and systemic inequality. We are oak trees, as my Nana used to say, who have endured and survived the horribleness that comes from living life as a Black person in America. I am confident that we will survive Donald Trump, the rise of White supremacy, and this ongoing cycle of violence that seems to have once become a part of our city. This is what life looks like when you are Black, and in so many ways, it is what it looks like when you are Black in Baltimore City. If you were born and raised here, then you know what it means to fight for survival. For some of us, who moved here later in life, we have learned over time that this is a city that experiences and has experienced incredible moments of joy and sorrow.

Søren Kierkegaard once said that life is best understood backward, but it must be experienced forward. The same, can be said about mourning—understood backwards but experienced forward. After years of mourning the countless deaths that have happened around this city, one would think that the reasons why and the solutions for would simply emerge. We are at the start of another school year with approximately 286 deaths under our belt. It has been a brutal summer and for many of us, the start of school will hopefully trigger a reduction in violence. Violence has become our new reality as research shows that one out of every 2,000 residents has been killed, the majority of which are young and Black, and shot in broad daylight. These are not scary fantasies that play out in the middle of the night; they are happening right before our eyes. They are sons, our grandparents, and our neighbors—and we are being called to do something, to say something.

In Baltimore City, which is now considered to be one of the most lethal of America's largest cities, the Mothers of Murdered Sons & Daughters, Inc. (MOMS) have decided that silence is not a solution, it is not the answer, and it will not stop the grip of violence that has once again found a way to slip in and slide its death grip around the neck of our city. MOMS, a Baltimore-based non-profit that is engaged in violence-prevention advocacy and support services for families victimized by homicide, has decided to be that voice crying out in the wilderness for change and for intervention.

Founded by Daphne Alston, whose son Tarik Sharif Alston, was fatally shot and killed in 2008, MOMS considers it their mission to speak out for those who cannot speak out for themselves, to force city government to solve this problem, and to find ways to invest in the lives of Black children as previous generations have done. They are not the only ones in the city who are concerned, but they represent a unique group. Most of the members are moms whose son or daughter was killed in Baltimore City. It is an intimate group. They do not recruit, they do not want new members, and when you do join, it is probably because your life has been forever changed. Meetings are run like support groups, with moms sharing their stories and their memories. There is a lot of handholding and tears and hugs and advocacy planning. They want the city to change. They want MOMS to be a group that is no longer needed. They are putting a face and a story to the names and numbers of victims. They are reminding us that the crime and violence in our city are directly connected to a crisis that is happening within the Black communities.

They are working hard to help end the plague of homicide in the Black communities, to change the social attitudes and conditions which serve to promote violence, and to provide ongoing support to mothers and families directly impacted by murder and homicide. They are demanding solutions rather than more explanations. Much of how young Black men in Baltimore resolve conflict is determined by individuals whose lives are well informed by violence and disparity. Their decision-making has been molded by context that has been developed in their community's time-worn narratives of pain, suffering, getting by and in many cases, simply getting over. For these communities, the War on Drugs, was personal, resulting in relentless attacks on their community by the law. In further exploring this reality, it is no wonder that Baltimore City became a fertile ground for the "Stop Snitching" campaign. This campaign, whether you agree with it or not, gave voice to a very pragmatic understanding that selling drugs put food on the table, paid college tuition, bought clothes and shoes, kept the water and the heat on, and provided bail money. It was a complicated network, Street Economics 101. Selling drugs also bought respect and spoke to a moral ambivalence, developed in

Black communities with few opportunities for lawful economic gain. This is real life, the stories behind the numbers. The moms are from these communities. They understand the context of this crisis and most importantly, as no other stakeholder in the discussion of homicide, these moms are the most informed about the pain left in homicide's wake. They are the ones who have been left behind to heal, to mourn, to speak out and to declare that homicide in Baltimore City is a community epidemic and a national health crisis. The White gaze does not define us, but our actions do. If we want our communities to heal, we must do like MOMS and work to make it happen.

Yes, donald trump is a racist

7/18/2019

When I was younger, my Nana used to say that there were some things in life that were undeniably true: The earth was going to spin. Nothing was certain but death and taxes. It was hard to be a Black woman in the South. She would shake her head and tell me that when things were undeniably true, the facts were so overwhelming that any attempt to argue against them would prove both futile and useless. I have kept her list and have added to it over the years: Voting is a civic duty. Black lives do matter. White supremacy is a clear and present danger. And, most recently, Donald Trump is a racist, bigoted xenophobe. I have never been surer of this than I am at this moment. He has actively and consistently used his platform to promote messages of racial division, intolerance, and hatred. He is a powerful and dangerous man and has never attempted to hide it. His racism is not new. His xenophobia and bigotry are not new. His hatred for Black and Brown people and his blatant disregard for women is not new. According to a recent article in The Atlantic ("An Oral History of Trump's Bigotry"), Trump has been actively promoting a racist and separatist agenda since 1973, when the Justice

Department filed charges against him for alleged acts of racial bias at his family's real-estate company. Over the years, as his platform has grown—from real estate to television to the Oval Office—and he has become more steadfast in his resolve to discredit, endanger, offend, and eliminate people of color, people with disabilities, and children.

This past weekend was another textbook example of what power looks like in the hands of a racist megalomaniac. On Sunday morning, as thousands of people braced themselves for the planned Immigration and Customs Enforcement (ICE) raids, Trump chose to focus his attention on the ongoing spat between House Speaker Nancy Pelosi and Representatives Alexandria Ocasio-Cortez, Rashida Tlaib, Ayanna Pressley, and Ilhan Omar ("The Squad," as they have come to be known). He took to Twitter and shared his racist, bigoted, xenophobic ramblings with the world. He stated that all the Representatives came from "countries whose governments are a complete and total catastrophe" and that they should "go back and help fix the totally broken and crime infested places." What was most disturbing about his asinine assertion is that three of them were born in America, and the other, like his mother, is a naturalized citizen. Even though they are as American as he is, because they are women of color, in his eyes, they are not.

His statements though dangerous and divisive were not surprising. As expected, the reaction was swift as everyone on the left, from politicians to entertainers to faith leaders, condemned his comments. When confronted (and possibly because the Republican base had been so silent), Trump simply doubled down and held firm. His words were a hollow reminder that in the perfect American narrative, access to the table and claims to this nation still only belong to White men. It is a classic argument as old as slavery and as dangerous as White supremacy.

It is the reason why White men first put on hoods to terrorize Black people and why they proceeded to lynch over 4,000 of them between 1877 and 1950. It is the thread that was used to hold Jim Crow together and the grout that was laid to help build and expand the New Jim Crow. It is what led White men to burn down both the Rosewood community and Black Wall Street and why it took so long to force this country to integrate. Trump knows that ever since the election of Barack Obama and the browning of America, there is a growing number of angry, disgruntled White people who believe that they are both losing both this country and their place in the world.

I believe that we have reached a racial tipping point in which people are going to have to choose which side they are going to support. If they decide to stand with Trump, then they are taking a stand against freedom, justice, diversity, and everything that we stand for and believe in as a nation. There is no middle ground. What is undeniably true is that our president is a racist, bigoted xenophobe, and anyone who supports him is probably one as well.

White supremacy is an ever-present danger

6/27/2019

In 1642, 312 years before the beginning of the modern civil rights era, the first documented Black protest happened in this country. Eleven enslaved men and women petitioned for and won their freedom and land from the Council of New Netherland (later renamed New York). Since then, as laws designed to restrict our rights began to be enacted, we have continued to organize, petition, fight and die for our freedom. We know what it is like to have to face the full power of Whiteness and not be moved or cowered into defeat. It is important to note that the desire to be free—to be equal and to be unrestricted in movement and opportunity—has always been present in this country, in the hearts and minds of Black people. Struggle is as much a part of our American experience as racism and Whiteness, the twin cousins of White supremacy that flow from and into one another. White supremacy is exhausting. It is dangerous, and it is frightening. It as a thread that is woven into the fabric of our country, and even if we pull on it, unless we are willing to pull the entire fabric apart, we will never be free from it.

In the past week alone, we have had multiple reminders of how tightly stitched the fabric is and has always been: from mourning the Charleston Nine (four years ago this week, they were murdered in their church by a White supremacist) to watching videos of police officers pulling their weapons on unarmed Black men, women, and children. It is painful, but it is a part of the lived experience of what it means to be Black in America during a time when Whiteness is being coddled and protected. As a researcher and a Black woman, I am often struck by the unique ways that Whiteness is used as both a shield and a battering ram. It happened during my father's generation as they fought to integrate this country, and it is happening now during my son's generation as they are fighting to make Black lives matter to everyone.

In the past month, I conducted an unofficial poll asking persons not of color whether they were aware of or familiar with any racial oppression in the United States within the last 100 years. I found that, across the board, the only racial moment that felt comfortable talking about was the March on Washington. Many of them mentioned Black Lives Matter, and when I asked them to elaborate, they were unable to do so. They went through a litany of names and slogans (from "Hands Up, Don't Shoot" to "I Can't Breathe"), but they could not talk about where the movement was now, what it has accomplished, or why it was still relevant. What is interesting is that if we just do the math, 100 years ago, we were living in a country where there was legal segregation. Throughout the South, Black and White folks were separated and were reminded daily that one race was superior, and the other was inferior. It was as simple as a porcelain water fountain versus a stone one, eating on the inside of a restaurant versus ordering your food from a backdoor in the alley, and, paying your money and getting on the front of the bus versus paying your money at the front door and then getting off and getting back on at the back door. At the same time, when you look at today's landscape, from Charlottesville to Ferguson, so much remains unchanged.

White supremacy is at the heart of all that remains unchanged and, in some ways, unchallenged. It is the thread that for so long has been used to hold this country together. It is what we are fighting against even if we cannot name it. It is that sinking feeling that Black and Brown folks get when something happens in which they are denigrated or overlooked or ignored, and they cannot verbalize what happened, but they can feel it in every cell of their body. In the last 100 years, we have seen people leaning in and forcing this country to live up to the creed laid out in our foundational documents. We have seen people willing to die or go to jail or be ostracized or Blackballed because they are drawing a line in the sand and saying not anymore, not on my watch.

We have seen changes over the last 100 years, changes that have worked to either completely end oppression or push it back. We need to understand that these changes happened because folks were willing to lean in; they were willing to bend their privilege; they were willing, to be honest, and admit that oppression and racism exists—even if it is not happening to them. Dr. King, in his "Letter from a Birmingham Jail," said it best: I have almost reached the regrettable conclusion that the Negro's great stumbling block in his stride toward freedom is not the White Citizen's Councilor or the Ku Klux Klan, but the White moderate, who is more devoted to "order" than to justice; who prefers a negative peace which is the absence of tension to a positive peace which is the presence of justice; who constantly says, "I agree with you in the goal you seek, but I cannot agree with your methods of direct action"; who paternalistically believes he can set the timetable for another man's freedom; who lives by a mythical concept of time and who constantly advises the Negro to wait for a "more convenient season." When someone says that there has not been any racial oppression in this country or that White supremacy has ended, everyone with a pen and a voice must speak out because as James Baldwin reminds us, history is not the past. It is the present. We carry our history with us. We are our history.

America (still) has a
White problem

8/15/2019

In 1965, President Lyndon Baines Johnson, in response to the violent racial attacks that were happening throughout the country, stated that the problem this country was facing was neither a Negro problem nor a Southern problem; it was an American problem. Speaking before a Joint Session of Congress, Johnson argued that this nation had to work together to overcome the "crippling legacy of bigotry and injustice." He was preparing Congress (and the world) to receive his Bill (which would later become the 1965 Voting Rights Act) that was designed to eliminate illegal barriers that prevented Black people from exercising their legal right to vote. Unfortunately, by laying the problem at the foot of America *writ large*, Johnson did what so many presidents had done before, and after him, he let White people off the hook. This blamelessness is what has allowed White people—from plantation owners to members of the KKK to White nationalists—to act with impunity and to go forward believing that they are acting in the best interest of this country.

This denial by White people of a Black person's right to vote, which included imposing poll taxes and literacy tests, along with threats of and actual acts of violence, was not a new problem. It was not a Negro problem. It was a White problem, and it had been a White problem since the first 20 Africans arrived in this country in 1619. Although it is not known whether they were enslaved or indentured servants, this ambiguity about the legal and social status of Black people in this country naturally lent itself to open-ended questions and debates around citizenship. What does it mean to be an American? Who has the right to claim this country as their own? These are not easy questions to answer in a country that is still wrestling with both the legacy of slavery and the brutal slaughter, mistreatment, and forced relocation of Native people. It is hard to answer while living in a country whose history is replete with stories of public lynchings and beatings, acts of White domestic terror, and rape, designed to frighten Black people into submission by reminding them, repeatedly, that America is not their home and will never be home to them. Black people are still fighting to be recognized, fighting to be seen, fighting to prove to White people that our lives, just like their lives, matter. Racism and oppression and White nationalism have never been Black problems; they have been and will continue to be—until they are recognized and dealt with—White problems.

I thought about this earlier this week when my family visited the Lorraine Motel. I spent the morning ambling through the exhibits, vacillating between feeling great anguish and overwhelming anger. I came upon an elderly Black couple, beautiful and dignified, walking slowly, backs slightly bent, heads held high. They stopped at each exhibit, speaking to each other in hushed tones, dabbing their eyes with White linen handkerchiefs. At the Montgomery Bus Boycott, they boarded the bus and placed their hands gently on the shoulder of the statue of Rosa Parks. When they walked past the bus from the Freedom

Rides, the man smiled as tears ran down his face. I never bothered them or spoke to them or tried to rush past them; I just smiled whenever I caught their eyes. I sat down at the exhibit for *Brown v. Board of Education*, thinking about the courage of the Little Rock Nine and Ruby Bridges, and I could not stop myself from weeping. I felt a gentle hand rub on my back, and when I looked up, the woman, with a smile on her face and tears in her eyes, caught my eye and nodded her head. At the Selma to Montgomery March exhibit, I stood next to them as the man read the words of President Johnson. When he finished reading, he looked at his wife and said, "It wasn't a Negro problem or an American problem; it was a White problem." She laughed and said, "It still is." As they walked away, all I could think about was that Johnson and this couple were both right: all the racial issues that we are struggling with are White problems, but because this country belongs to all of us, they are American problems, and it will take all of us to solve them.

America is a divided nation

12/8/2016

America is a divided nation. This is not new information or a startling revelation. It is simply a fact that clearly defines where we are at this moment. This country has in so many ways, always been divided: it happened when slavery was legalized, when women were not allowed to vote; when Jim Crow became the law of the land, and when our economy began to grow on the backs and labor of the poor and the enslaved. Our public schools are divided and unequal, and our communities, particularly here in Baltimore, are deeply segregated. We are a microcosm of America. It is divided and so are we. Fifty years ago this week, the National Advisory Commission on Civil Disorders that was organized by Lyndon B. Johnson released the Kerner Commission Report. It was organized in 1967, after the intense racial riots and unrest swept through the country, and it was named after the chairperson, Otto Kerner, Jr. They were charged with answering three questions: What happened? Why did it happen? What can be done to prevent it from happening again and again? It was a time of immense contradictions, as this occurred only a few years after the passage of the Civil Rights Act of 1964, which outlawed discrimination and prohibited unequal application of voter registration requirements, racial segregation in schools, employment, and public accommodation; and the Voting Rights Act of 1965, which prohibited racial discrimination in voting.

When the Report was released in 1968, it noted that our nation was "moving toward two societies, one Black, one White—separate and unequal." They concluded that this division was the result of failed government housing, decent education and social-service policies, and the narrative that had been created by mainstream media who reported the news while looking out from a White world with a "white man's eyes and a white perspective." They suggested that the main cause for urban violence was White racism and that White America needed to fully and completely shoulder most of the responsibility for the rioting and rebellion that was happening across the country. Statistics for 1967 alone showed that over 1800 people had been injured (mostly Black people) and 83 people had been killed. The property damages were valued at upwards of $100 million dollars in over 123 cities.

The Kerner Commission then outlined some broad solutions to promoting racial integration, which included creating more jobs and job training programs, establishing decent housing, and increasing financial aid to Black communities. Although Johnson rejected the report because they did not praise his anti-poverty program, conversations started taking place across the country, as Black and White communities tried to work together to find solutions to bridge the divide. Thirty years later, in 1998, the Eisenhower Foundation commissioned a follow-up report, and they found that there was more poverty in America and that it was "deeper, Blacker and browner than before" and more concentrated in the cities, which had become "America's poorhouses." Even with all the conversations and policies, the laws and the direct intervention, America was still a racially and economically divided nation.

It is now 2018 and even though we elected the nation's first Black president (twice) and we have seen the rise of the Movement for Black Lives and the impact of the work that many of us have done to help create a more diverse, open, accountable, and inclusive society, it is clear that we are back at the beginning, and we are as divided today as we were fifty years ago. We are well into the world that Donald Trump has created, and despite the protests and marches, and ongoing pushback against him, with every decision, tweet, or comment that he makes, it is clear that America is more divided, more White, more racist, more classist and exclusive, more misogynistic, and more frightening. Adding to that is the stark realization that the recommendations of the 1968 Kerner Commission, which included America pouring billions of dollars into the urban cities to prevent further racial violence and polarization, were never implemented. It should not come as a surprise that many in our country believe that we are really two nations deeply divided by race and class.

It is clear that these feelings are grounded in reality as a new report, "Healing Our Divided Society: Investing in America Fifty Years After the Kerner Report," released earlier this week, notes that "there are far more people who are poor now than was true 50 years ago. Inequality of income is worse." This work, which included input from Black people, Latinos, Native Americans, and women, concludes that since 1968, the country has not only had a widening gap in poverty, but there also has been a noted and concentrated lack of or reversal of progress. In other words, we are getting worse, and the lines of division are getting wider. They also offered suggestions, similar in scope to the ones that were offered in 1968: spending more money on early childhood education, increasing the minimum wage to $15 by 2024, more regulatory oversight over mortgage leaders to prevent predatory lending, establishing community policing that works in concert with nonprofits in inner-city communities, and adding more job-training programs in an era of automation and emerging technologies. They also called on the mainstream media to hire more people of color to cover and report the news, particularly in communities of color. Fifty years later, the country is getting worse, but the solutions, the way to turn the tide, have not changed. My hope is that this time, we will not let them forget. We will not let them dismiss the report. And we will not let them continue to move us farther away from where we want to be: one nation, one society, inclusive, diverse, and equal.

Repeal the damn Second Amendment

9/13/2019

4:20 a.m.: It is quiet outside, and this is my daily soul check time. I slowly open my eyes, without getting up, and ask myself the same question. Do I remember who I used to be before I became the person that I am now? I remind myself to be still, to breathe, and, to remember how I got over. I tell myself that I am the descendant of people who chose to survive. I get up slowly and make my way to the mirror. I stand in front of it and remind myself that I am the hope and the dream of women who fought to both have dreams and keep their hopes alive. I sigh deeply as I think about how my grandmother used to lift me up on her shoulders so that I could see all her land. She was a proud Black woman who taught me to lift my head, to never look over my shoulder, and, in the face of weapons and racism, not to blink or turn away. I think about her every morning, and even though she taught me to brave, the reality is that today, I am a coward. I live in fear and what scares me, what keeps me up at night, is the growing sense that at any moment, on any day, in any given space, my sons could be shot and killed.

We live in a country that has more guns than people. It is a place where we average a mass shooting per day while our politicians do not seem to have the testicular fortitude needed to repeal the damn Second Amendment. It is clear, as Dr. King once said, that we are all tied together in an inescapable network of mutuality and responsibility, so we are all plagued and haunted by the same demons, some real and some imagined. Every morning as I look into my mirror, I see myself through a very narrow lens: I am a Black mother who has chosen to live and raise my sons in Baltimore City. Every day, my demons, my nightmares, play out in the lives and stories of women all around me. When I read the stories of children and women being shot, my heart aches, and my breath slows down. This is a moment where the broken-down souls of heavy-laden mothers rarely get a chance to mourn. In this country, we are more likely to die from gun violence than from many leading causes of death combined with some 11,000 people in the US killed in firearm assaults each year. As of September 3rd, according to data from the nonprofit Gun Violence Archive, there have been 283 mass shootings this year in this country. Here in Baltimore City, where we regularly deal with reports of triple and quadruple shootings and homicides, 218 people have been shot and killed. This represents a 25% increase in shootings and sets us on a pace to exceed 300 murders for the fifth year in a row.

It is exhausting because there have been too many bodies, too many bullets, too many marches, and too many hashtags to properly mourn, so we bury them somewhere inside of ourselves, and then we rise--again. Less than two weeks ago, as I drove my youngest son to fencing practice, I turned onto a side street and rode past three men, two White and one Asian. They were laughing and playing with a rifle, and when we rode by them, the Asian man raised the gun and pointed it at my car. Since they were standing on my son's side, I put my arm across him. Although

I knew, somewhere in the back of my brain, my arm would not save him, I could not stop myself. I felt helpless as if I was drowning in my own nightmares. All I could do was grit my teeth, tears in my eyes, and keep moving forward. I was scared. I felt alone. I felt like no one was coming to save me, coming to save us. I reached out to a therapist friend who told me that during those moments when I feel most afraid, I should say to myself things like, "I am safe. He is safe. We are safe." Unfortunately, every time I do so, the realist in me whispers the words, "for now" because unless we repeal the damn Second Amendment and get rid of our obsession with guns, we will never be safe.

Dear racist White people, your time is up

5/15/2019

A few nights ago, while my sons were sitting and doing their homework, I stood at the doorway, and I just looked at them. I thought about how much I loved them and about what it takes for me to send them out into a world with people like you, the ones that do not value them or see their genius and their brilliance. I watched as they struggled with their physics and double checked their calculus, and I thought about the letter that James Baldwin wrote to his nephew in 1963 when he told him that, "You were born where you were born and faced the future that you faced because you were Black and for no other reason. The limits to your ambition were thus expected to be settled. You were born into a society which spelled out with brutal clarity and in as many ways as possible that you were a worthless human being. You were not expected to aspire to excellence. You were expected to make peace with mediocrity." I thought about this and had to stop myself from crying or screaming because, with all the work that we have done to make this country better, Black children should no longer have to make peace with mediocrity or failure, suffering or poverty. They should not have to make peace with racism and injustice. They should not have to think about being harassed by the police or being called the n-word by their teachers. They should not have to worry that they will get arrested because they are selling water, mowing a lawn, or ordering food.

I stood there and realized that no matter how far we have come, this country still has a long way to go before it can both recognize and practice equity and social justice. We are amid some very dark days. These are the days that my grandmother warned me about when she said that the real battle in this country is the work to change the hearts and minds of racist White people. I used to believe that America had a race problem because we were unwilling to do the hard work to bring about the changes that needed to happen. I have since come to a different conclusion. America does not have a race problem; it has a problem with racists because they refuse to recognize or accept how much this country has changed and how much they need to change. They do not realize that their time is up.

Here is what they need to understand: racism is an ouroboros (a beast) and all the tenets that come with it and help to maintain it—from White complicity to White privilege, White nationalism to White supremacy—must be destroyed. If not, then it will regenerate. It will be reborn, and it will help to shape the next generation. Therefore, it feels like we are fighting the same battles and no matter how much things have changed, things have remained the same. I believe that no amount of marching or praying, crying or mourning, teaching or talking will bring about the change we need to see. The system itself must be dismantled. We must drag this beast of racism and everything that comes with it to the altar of Whiteness and sacrifice it there.

I thought about all of this as I looked at my sons, realizing that this is a battle that they now must fight because my generation (and the generations that have come before me) have failed. I hope and believe that they will succeed. Khalil Gibran once said that "Our children are not our children. They are the sons and the daughters of Life's longing for itself. They come through us but not from us, and though they are with us yet, they belong not to us." I have taught my sons how to fight. They are sober-minded and self-aware. They have the tools: their pens are their swords, and their words are their weapons. They are well-trained, and they are brilliant. They know that they are the hope and the dream of the slaves, and because of this, I know that they will win.

Has America gone to hell?

8/31/2017

On Thursday, April 4, 1968, only a couple of hours before he would be assassinated, Martin Luther King Jr. sat in his room, working on his Sunday sermon, aptly titled "Why America May Go to Hell." It was a speech that would never be finished. After years of fighting for integration, it was obvious to the folks who knew him and to those who were listening closely to his speeches that the King of 1967 who said that White people's belief in the fairness of America **was "a fantasy of self-deception and comfortable vanity" was a much different** man than the King of 1955 who led the Montgomery Bus Boycott and told us to "love our enemies and be good to them." Something had changed him. Perhaps it was the constant arrests or the bombing of his home or the feeling that he was fighting a war that he could not win. In either case, his tone had become much harsher, and his attitude seemed to be less tolerant while waiting for racist White people to change. He had expanded his criticism of America beyond the issue of race and had begun to confront poverty, the economic power structure, and the Vietnam War. He was building an interracial coalition, and it was probably taking everything out of him.

There are stories of him being depressed, not sleeping, suffering from migraines, and of confiding in Harry Belafonte about his concerns that we were fighting long and hard to integrate into a "burning house."

This is the Dr. King that I was taught about, the radical one who would have supported Black Lives Matter and who would have challenged White supremacy. The same man who in 1967 asked the question that I have been asking myself since Charlottesville, "**Why does White America delude itself, and how does it rationalize the evil it retains?**" The question was relevant back then and it is even more relevant now. It is a question that demands an answer, and it can only be answered by White America. I have received countless emails from White people asking me what they should be doing right now, I would argue that wrestling with this question and attempting to answer it should be somewhere near the top of their to-do list. In reading through his sermon notes, King was not arguing that America should go to hell but that it might, based upon its inability to end racism, materialism, and militarism. It was a speech that America still needs to hear.

Sixty-two years ago this week, Emmett Till was taken from his home and brutally murdered by White men. There was no justice in that case, and for many, who have lost their loved ones to state-sanctioned police violence or White vigilantes, there is still no peace. Fifty-four years ago this week, at the March on Washington, John Lewis challenged us to march through this country until we splintered the segregated South into "a thousand pieces" and put it back together in the "image of God and democracy." Segregation has legally ended, and the signs have come down, but our country is more divided than ever. Forty-eight years ago, King argued that the U.S. government was "the greatest purveyor of violence in the world today." A year later, the man that the FBI deemed the most dangerous man in America was assassinated. Three weeks ago, Heather Hayer—in a country that has elected a Black man twice to be its president and is now more racially diverse than it has ever been—was killed while protesting the alt-right in Charlottesville, VA.

We find ourselves once again back at a moment of reckoning when we must realize that tomorrow is today, and we are confronted with the fierce urgency of now. I would add that this fierce urgency requires us to do more acting than reflecting and more action than conversation. We must organize and focus our energies and our attention on fighting White supremacy. It is the ugly beast that always rears its head during Black Reconstruction. It is an obverse reminder that there still some White people who are willing to sacrifice themselves on the altar of Whiteness to keep the pillars of separation erected. American enslavement lasted for 267 years, but the remnants of it—the belief that certain people are superior and certain folks are inferior—have remained with us, in our statutes, in our statues, in our policies, in our practices, in our nation-wide history curricula and in the hearts and minds of some people. Forty-nine years ago, Dr. King wondered if America, due to its inability to change and grow and be better, might go to hell; I sometimes wonder—when I look around at all this hatred and anger and violence and destruction and poverty and pessimism—whether we are already there.

Should God bless America?

6/30/2017

My entire life has been centered on the belief that God wants to bless America and that he is only waiting for us to ask. Growing up as the daughter of a Southern Black Baptist minister, my life was filled with church services, communion, and prayer. I learned early how to get down on my knees at the end of every day and ask for forgiveness and ask God to bless my family and America. My dad is a veteran, having served during the Vietnam War, and he believed that we needed to remember that America was always primed to be attacked and that it was our prayers for her that kept her safe.

He was also raised in Jim Crow South Carolina and had been actively involved in the Civil Rights Movement, and he taught me that the America that we were asking God to bless was not the one that we saw in front of us, but it has the potential for what she could someday become. He said that when he would get arrested or spit upon or he was called the n-word, he would silently ask God to bless America despite the hatred and the inequality. When the Rev. Martin Luther King and President John F. Kennedy were assassinated, he told me that the only thing that got him through those days was prayer and asking God repeatedly to overlook the sins of this country and bless us anyway.

We lived in a small Black community in Washington, DC, where most of

my teachers were members of my church and when they spoke, in my mind, they had the authority of God behind them. Every morning, from 1st to 8th grade, we had to stand and recite the Pledge of Allegiance. We were "under God," we were "indivisible," and we did provide "liberty and justice for all." As a young child, it made sense to me. America was the center of the world, morally balanced and uniquely charged with the task of saving and protecting the planet. In history class, my teachers buried us in stories of dead White men, the vaunted Christian forefathers, who worked hard to craft a more perfect union, without teaching us that they were racist, sexist, classist slave holders. We never talked about what or who was missing from these great American tales of courage and valor, never questioned the validity and reliability of these stories. We simply accepted them as the truth, praying for and pledging ourselves to a nation that denied our humanity, that fought a war to keep us enslaved, that set up laws to keep us separate and that was comfortable lynching, beating, and oppressing us.

I was 5 years old the first time a president ended a speech by calling on God

to bless America. It was 1973, President Richard Nixon, while dealing with the Watergate scandal, ended a speech by saying, "Tonight, I ask for your prayers to help me in everything I do throughout the days of my presidency. God bless America, and God bless each and every one of you." This was a watershed moment when God entered the realm of politics and became both a shield and a weapon. As American citizens, how do we begin to question the actions of our leaders when they invoke the name of God and call upon him to bless us? This phrase was not used again until Ronald Reagan, and since then every president, has called on God publicly to bless this country. I know that God can, but I am wondering if he should. Should God bless America, a place where economic and social freedom only exist in the lives of a privileged few, a place where women and girls are routinely sexually assaulted, a place where Black and Brown people must proclaim that their lives matter? A place where the current president is, by his own words and deeds, a bigot and a demagogue who tweets out hatred on a daily basis and whose election (America's Whitelash moment) ushered in a new age of divisiveness, racism, xenophobia, and hatred—a man who ends every speech by calling on God to bless America.

By God's own words, recorded in his holy Bible—where he calls on us to

love our neighbor as we love ourselves, to practice radical hospitality, to be the good Samaritan, to shoulder one another's burdens, to welcome the prodigal children home, to be kind and gentle and long suffering and peaceful, and to be slow to anger and quick to listen—America is not a country that deserves his blessing. But then I think of my father and remember that we pray not for the ossified, divided America that this country is at this moment, but for the possibility of what she can become. And so, I will continue to ask God to bless America, while also advocating every day to change her.

We don't have to win;
we just have to hold on

3/26/2022

Four nights ago, I sent out a tweet praying that the people of Ukraine prevail against the relentless attack from President Putin and the Russian Army. I said that I was praying for them to win. I received a reply in just a few minutes that stopped me in my tracks: "We don't have to win; we just have to hold on." Since then, I have been thinking about this sentiment, this idea, and this prayer. It reminded me of my father, who once taught me to hold on to the broken pieces. I thought about my grandmother, who once said faith was holding on even when everything in you tells you to let go. It made me think about my ancestors, enslaved men, and women, who had never known or tasted freedom, but they were confident that someone in their line would know how it felt to be free if they just held on.

Dr. Martin Luther King Jr. once said, "We must build dikes of courage to *hold* back the flood of fear." I always believed that he was telling us to build it in faith since we wouldn't know whether it would hold until it was built and tested. I sat in my chair and thought about how I am here today because my ancestors held on and blazed a trail of excellence and brilliance. I stand on their shoulders, grateful for all that they have done. They have shown all of us how to walk with our heads held up high, knowing that we may not see the end, but we will get there, and we need to get there together. They have shown us the importance of knowing our place in the line.

From Ukraine to America, people worldwide are standing at the crossroads of freedom and equality. We are at an interesting time in American history because the arc of the moral universe that Dr. King and Minister Theodore Parker once wrote about is still bending. It may not be bending as quickly as we would like, but it is still bending. "The universe," as King once said, "is on the side of justice," but it is evident that justice is taking a long time to get here.

Before my oldest son left for college, I told him that it was a privilege to be able to attend college to pursue his dreams and his degree. I told him he was a part of Franz Shubert's Unfinished Symphony—as college will bring him into a conversation that has been going on before he arrived and will continue after he leaves. His challenge is to leave the conversation a little bit better than how he found it. I said you must decide who you are going to be, what kind of world you want to live in, and what you are willing to sacrifice to help create this world.

I told him a story I once heard about a little girl, whose mother gave her a 1000-piece puzzle of the world and told her to take her time and put the world together.

The mother figured that this would take a couple of days and would occupy her daughter's time. In mere minutes her daughter was finished, and her mother wanted to know how she could make the world fit together in such a short period of time. The little girl said that her father told her that on the other side of the puzzle pieces was a picture of a little girl, and if she just focused on putting the little girl together in the right way, then the world would come together. I then asked him, are you putting your puzzle pieces together in the right way? Are you where you are supposed to be? Do you understand that you do not have to win; you have to hold on? We have a great responsibility because as the arc is bending, those of us who know the history or have lived the history or have studied the history must be charged with the responsibility of teaching the history.

We must share our knowledge to ensure that the generations to come will not continue to be destroyed because they have not learned their history or, worse yet, have rejected it. We must do our part to spark their genius—the genius that Dr. Carter G. Woodson, the founder of ASALH and Negro History Week, was talking about in his book, *The Mis-Education of the Negro*—and as we do that, we must also seek to spark that genius in ourselves as well. As Dr. King wrote in his *Letter from a Birmingham Jail*, we must hold on because we are all caught up in an "inescapable network of mutuality, tied in a single garment of destiny. Whatever affects one directly affects all indirectly." After reading this letter, who could be silent and risk having their silence mistaken for complicity? We read that letter today and forget that it is calling us to do something, to go farther than we ever thought possible. It is calling us to realize that our stories are connected and intricately tied to the stories that are being told around the world. The suffering in Kyiv is tied to the suffering in Syria and the current struggle to free Brittany Griner is just as important as the struggle that once took place to help free Liu Xiaobo. Injustice anywhere—whether in Florida, Baltimore, Turkey, Sudan, or Sandy Hook—is a threat to justice everywhere—a statement as true today as it was when King first wrote them. What we know to be true is that as a collective body, committed to peace and justice, we do not have to win; we just have to be able to hold on.

Today, what to a Black person is the Fourth of July?

7/7/2017

I had a moment during Sunday service, when my pastor asked us to stand, turn toward the American flag and recite the Pledge of Allegiance. I cringed as everyone quickly stood, placed their hands over their hearts, and proceeded to recite the Pledge, without question and without hesitation. I sat there fighting against my desire to stand and be obedient because I knew that as a Black person in America, I could not pledge my allegiance to this racist nation or to our bigoted president. In psychology, they call this moment cognitive dissonance, which happens when a person is struggling with at least two contradictory beliefs, ideas, or values. I am a descendant of enslaved people who fought to survive in America and war veterans who died while fighting to protect America. I am a walking contradiction where my American racist values and my Black consciousness and pride are constantly warring against one another. W.E.B. Du Bois called it double consciousness, an oppressive way of viewing and judging yourself, as a Black person, through the eyes of a racist White society.

I thought about all of this as the Pledge gave way to the singing of "My Country 'Tis of Thee," because I believe that this America, this bastion of White supremacy, is not my ideal home. It is not where I feel safe or where I feel like I belong. I am the Sankofa bird who flies forward across this red, White, and blue landscape with rivers that run deep with the blood of innocent Black and Brown people, while hopelessly keeping my head turned in search of something else, of somewhere else. This feeling of Black restlessness, despair, frustration, and anger is not new. It always feels like it is our blood that is on the leaves and at the roots, fertilizing the soil that feeds the American dream of White exceptionalism. We have long felt like we did not belong here. But we endured. We stayed and we survived. But still, in church I wanted to stand, as this is what I have been taught to do by my father and obviously expected to do by my pastor. I wanted to be obedient and follow the rules.

I really want to be proud of my country and to celebrate her independence. I want to answer Frederick Douglass's question, "What to the Slave is the Fourth of July?" and tell him that although it has taken us 165 years, we have finally arrived. I want to say that the Fourth of July is now our holiday for we have been embraced and counted as part of the American dream, that we have been allowed to fully participate in the democratic process and have seen the day when a person is judged by the content of their character and not the color of their skin. I want to say that we have gotten past the racist notion that skin color is more important than skills and talent, that we no longer shout that "Black Lives Matter," for we have gotten to a point where those types of questions (about who matters and who does not) have been settled and that we have realized that we are stronger together as one nation than we are apart.

I want to say that, but I cannot. I think of Philando Castile and Alton Sterling; Terence Crutcher and Korryn Gaines; John Crawford III and Eric Garner; Rekia Boyd and Aiyana Jones; Tamir Rice and Freddie Gray, and countless others. I think of their lives and of what we lost on the day that they were murdered. These are the moments when America—a beacon and shining light of White hope and pride—brutally reminds us that the Fourth of July is theirs and not ours, and as they celebrate, we must mourn. It is hard to pledge allegiance to a country that does not recognize your humanity. In 1852, Douglass noted that slavery was the great sin and shame in America; today it is oppression, and it is White supremacy, and it is injustice.

Five minutes before the Klan shows up

7/9/2020

As someone who grew up in Jim Crow South Carolina, my father likes to call himself a survivor. He looked White supremacy and racial hatred in the eye, and though he has not won, he wants to note that he has not lost, not yet. When I was in college, I asked him why he was convinced that he had not won. He said that winning, for Black folks, would only come when we could walk anywhere in this country and not be concerned that the color of our skin could mean the end of our lives.

My father remembers the days when they called him "boy" even though he was a man, of being dismissed and overlooked even when he followed the rules, and of hearing his mother cry when she realized that he had decided to fight back and not give way. Those types of decisions, he would say, are best made once you realize that you are willing to die to be free rather than live in fear under the thumb of Whiteness. My father's family carried pistols and shotguns whenever they rode into town. My grandfather used to sit on a pillow, and his pistol would be underneath, on the right side, in case he needed to grab it in a hurry. His sons, my father's brothers, would have shotguns on the floor near their feet. Nobody ever said it, but everybody knew that if the Klan confronted them, they were prepared to meet their Maker, standing up and fighting back.

Such was the reality of living in a southern county where performative Whiteness manifested itself through the law and daily acts of random domestic terror against Black people. It was not unusual for Black women to have a *kaffeeklatsch*, sharing horrific tales of lynchings and cross burnings over sweet potato pie and integrated coffee. It was not uncommon for Black households to keep an open Bible on the coffee table and a loaded shotgun at the door. My grandmother knew how to shoot. She knew how to steady her shoulder and set her arm so that her hands never wavered. She grew up on a farm, way down South, so she knew how to pick cotton, twist off a chicken's head, grab her shotgun, look White terror in the eye, and not look away. My father once told me that the best time to plant a tree was 50 years ago, and the best time to decide to fight against Whiteness was five minutes before the Klan showed up. Such decisions, he would say, must be made before you see the White sheets out your front window.

My father was 12 years old when they murdered Emmett Till in Money, Mississippi. He remembers how his mother and all the women at the church were weeping and wailing during Sunday church service. What kind of men, the pastor intoned, could look a boy in the eye and then torture him to death? How much effort would it take for us to love the hell out of White people's hearts and minds? My dad said the murder of Emmett Till changed everything. After that, Black boys were taught by their parents, who wanted to keep them alive, not to look White women in the eye, not to speak first, and not to be too excited once you spoke. It was the act of bearing witness to his friends learning how to give way that strengthened my father's resolve to fight. If I was going to die at the hands of Whiteness, he told me, I was prepared to do it standing up with my shotgun in my hand and a steely resolve in my eye. The summer before they heard about Emmett Till, my father said my grandmother used to sing a song around the house when she was cleaning up. He said she kept her voice real low, but sometimes when she thought she was alone, she would sing loud enough to catch the words: Black body swinging in the Southern breeze, Strange fruit hanging from the poplar trees. He said those were the days when she would ask his father to check the shotgun, and she would then tell the kids not to leave the front yard. Black boys, my father would say, should be able to roam free, explore and see the world, walk along with their friends, and dream aloud. We can never say that we have defeated Whiteness until this happens.

A few weeks ago, amid the worldwide protests for justice for Ahmaud Arbery, Breonna Taylor, George Floyd, and Rayshard Brooks, I called my father. We sat in silence, for a long time, on the phone. I told him that I did not know how to move forward and let my sons, his grandsons, fight for Black Lives and against Whiteness during a global pandemic. I felt stuck. The best time to decide to fight Whiteness, he reminded me, is five minutes before the Klan arrives. I have been thinking a lot about my father, his life, his words of wisdom and his decision to fight. He raised me to be a fighter. He taught me to speak first, look folks in the eye and be myself when I do it. I am the tree that he planted all those years ago. Before he hung up the phone, he said that the second-best time to fight Whiteness is right before you see the White sheets out your front window. You must fight and let them fight until we win or until we meet our Maker. In either case, we will do it standing up and fighting back.

9 minutes and 29 seconds

4/1/2021

Pictures of children in pain tend to haunt me. It is the wide-eyed look of either sheer terror or deep-rooted sadness that takes me out. I look at them and see myself during those moments after my father used his belt and his power to remind me that justice is never blind when the strong make the rules and mete out the punishment. It is the eyes, too old for the face, that make me wonder what it says about a country or a parent that treats its children, its future, this way.

I have seen so many pictures of children who were hungry or terrified or in pain, who were marching during the Birmingham Children's Campaign or trying to survive during Hitler's reign of terror. And children whose faces were captured on the edges of the pictures taken after Sandy Hook, after Marjory Stoneman Douglass, after the Baltimore Uprising—children who were comforting their mother at the funeral of Martin Luther King Jr. or saluting their father as his coffin slowly rode by. Children should be protected at all costs if we are to have a real shot at getting past the sin that wears us down. And when a society cannot or will not protect its children from racism, from police brutality, from White supremacy then.... (My hands are actually shaking as I write this, signs that childhood trauma experienced through a racial, gendered lens will also find a way back into your soul.)

It was the testimony of a 9-year-old on day two of the murder trial of Derek Chauvin that broke me. The child said that they watched Chauvin (a White police officer) keep his knee on George Floyd's neck (a Black man) even after the EMT workers repeatedly asked him to move. If, as the defense attorney stated, Chauvin was doing his job, then the killing of unarmed Black men, women and children is routine. It is expected and is as ordinary as stopping a speeding car or writing a parking ticket. Killing us, like animals in the street, acting as judge, juror, and executioner, is simply part of their job. As I read the child's testimony, I knew what they saw. I watched the video just once. I saw Mr. Floyd on the ground, struggling and gasping, crying, and trying to get up. I heard him scream, "I can't breathe," and I thought about Eric Garner, who was choked and killed by former New York City police officer Daniel Pantaleo who also screamed out with his dying breath that he could not breathe. Hell, when I watched both of those videos, six years apart, I could not breathe.

As Black people, these are the moments that weather us, that age us, that raise our *allostatic racial load*. In 1983, Bruce McEwan and Stellar wrote about the allostatic load, which is the general wear and tear on the body shaped by repeated or prolonged chronic stress. So, an increase in stress levels results in an increase in stress on the brain, and your health which then causes the body to begin to breakdown. As Black people in America, we are exposed to increased stress levels tied directly to racism, and I believe that we have more than just an allostatic load; we have an allostatic racial load. Our bodies are being weathered and aged because we are Black people living in a racist country. When we say that we cannot breathe, it is more than just trying to get air into our lungs. It is about trying to find spaces where we can be free from the stress that comes from living Blackness in a place where only Whiteness is supposed to exist.

I thought about all of that when I read the testimony of a 9-year-old child talking through 9 minutes and 29 seconds of pure horror.

For the first 4 minutes and 45 seconds, Mr. Floyd struggled, tried to get up, yelled out that he couldn't breathe and cried out for his mother. Chauvin and his brother officers did not move because when they were doing their job; they did not hear our cries of pain.

For the next 53 seconds, Mr. Floyd had multiple seizures, no words, just his body crying out in pain and Chauvin and his brother officers did not react because when they are doing their job; they do not see our pain.

For the final 3 minutes and 51 seconds, Mr. Floyd was utterly non-responsive, did not move, and Chauvin and his brother officers did not bat an eye because, when they are simply doing their job, they cannot comprehend that we are dying from the pain that they are inflicting upon us.

The video of this murder has been viewed over 1.4 billion times, 50 million times in the last few days alone. Racism is killing us. White supremacy is killing us. Whiteness is killing us. Do not look away because in this moment, like the 9-year-old that testified, your truth, your witness, your voice, your testimony are needed.

America is a racist country

9/30/2020

This is our American story, built on disillusion and disappointment, survival, and sacrifice. It is not a new story, nor is it for the faint of heart. America is a beast that prides itself on feeding off our pain. It is a red, White, and blue nightmare of a tale where Black and Brown people exist at the story's bleeding edge.

This is not new information for me, having grown up spending every summer in the backwoods of South Carolina. I came of age in the heart of the Confederacy, the first state to secede from the Union and the first territory to have African enslaved labor. Whenever we drove to Bamberg County to visit my great-grandmother, my Nana would always mention Lucas Vázquez de Ayllón's colony because she wanted me to understand that the Black man's struggle to be free from White rule is as much of a part of the American story as the struggle of the White man to be free from British rule.

During the school year, I lived in Washington, DC, Chocolate City, where I learned to say it loud that I am Black, and I am proud. As soon as school ended, my parents would pack us up and take us to South Carolina, where the malodorous aroma of racism hung in the air and choked us as soon as we crossed the state line. I used to dread going to the market with my Nana, listening as the White store owners, voices heavy with that cotton-stuffed Southern accent, were patronizingly polite with her.

I staged my first protest in South Carolina against that same store owner when he refused to remove his framed "Whites Only" sign from the front counter. I was seven years old when I was called the n-word, for the first time, by the father of my best friend, a young White boy who lived down the street. His father hated those "Yankee n-words" and used to boast about what he was going to do to them when the South rose again. When my friend told me that he hated them, I quickly said I hated them too. When I told my Nana, that was the last time I played with him, and it was at least four years before I found out why. She used to say that nobody is born a racist; they are raised on moonshine and White supremacy and molded and shaped on tales of Whiteness, hog maw, and fatback. It is the accent that gets me every time and brings back memories of pick-up trucks full of White boys driving near our home, calling us the n-word while spitting in our direction. South Carolina sits at the root of my anger and resentment.

Last week, at the Republican National Convention, when the former governor of South Carolina, Nikki Haley, said that America was not a racist country, my skin started to crawl. She said that she had been a Brown girl in a White world, but she has no idea of what it means to have been a Black girl in that same world. We probably passed one another on the street when we were growing up. When she spoke, I said then what I have said for as long as I can remember: South Carolina is a racist state, and America is a racist country.

I now say this with an increased sense of urgency because we are in a crisis where our country is burning from within. It is a moment when a global pandemic that has so far infected six million Americans and killed approximately 188,000 people is moving across this country, disproportionately impacting Black and Brown people, and revealing the deep cracks of racism, hypocrisy, and anger. We are seven months into trying to deal with and live through this novel coronavirus and 401 years into trying to end this war against the Black body (and against Black joy and Black agency and Black freedom and…). We are at a moment where Black Lives Matter has met COVID-19 and has laid bare to the world that the *faux* post-racial moment that many believed happened with the election of Barack Obama was merely a lie wrapped in a façade, masquerading as the truth. My Nana tried to tell them back then that "one election does not equality make."

America, she would often say, is racist to the core. This system oppresses us. It is the knee on our neck, holding us back, pinning us down, and making it so damn hard for us to breathe. Coretta Scott King said that freedom is never really won; you earn it and win it in every generation. And Ella Baker said that we who believe in freedom cannot rest. Angela Davis said you must act as if it were possible to radically transform the world, and you must do it all the time. My Nana, one of the first Black nurses in South Carolina, said that Black people are born fighting to breathe, and they must live fighting to survive. America *is* a racist country, but we will change it. It is a hellfire, but we will extinguish it. It is an ouroboros, but we will cut it off at the head. We will transform this country. We will transmogrify this country because, at this critical moment, as Assata Shakur once said, we have nothing (else) to lose but our chains.

Trump was a necessary evil

11/12/2020

Unlike 71 million Americans across this country, I voted against Donald Trump and against authoritarianism, fascism, xenophobia, and bigotry. When I voted, I did it to take a stand against hatred, White supremacy, and racism. Now to be clear, I have always intentionally voted *for* a candidate and not necessarily *against* one. In 2016, I voted *for* Hilary Rodham Clinton. In 2008 and 2012, I voted *for* Barack Obama. I did not even consider anyone else's platform because I was working *for* my candidate. The 2020 election season has been very different, filled with stress and tension, and shaped by anxiety and fear, not just in the United States but worldwide. The presidency of Trump has forced us to move from being mere observers of the political process to working actively shape it. We no longer just vote *for* a candidate; we now vote *against* one. My vote was a repudiation of Trump, and it felt good to get that vote, that single solitary act of resistance and defiance, off my chest. And even though I grew up voting, I felt the need to cry and celebrate after I dropped off my ballot.

Growing up, my father used to take me with him on Election

Day and talk to me about the people in our family who fought so that he (and one day, I) could vote. He would tell me stories about how Dr. King believed that our vote could transform America and how Malcolm X argued that changing this country would come down to the ballot or the bullet. Voting, he would say, was one of the few weapons we have to bring about change in this country, and I must wield my weapon responsibly. I thought about that when I ran for office in sixth grade. I wanted to be a crossing guard, and in my school, that was an elite elected position. My campaign slogan was "Vote for Someone You Trust to Do a Job That You Need." I think I was more excited about the campaign than the job. It was an enormous responsibility, and when I complained, my father reminded me that that I worked for people and should put their needs before my own. I never forgot that lesson, and I think about it every time I vote. I cast my ballot for someone I trust to do a job that I need. I have rejoiced when my candidate won and doubled down on my work when they lost. I did not take it personally; I just committed myself to work harder the next time. 2016 was different. I took Trump's victory as a moral affront to me and everybody in this country who believed in freedom and justice.

Before Trump's election, I used to get a little annoyed when I talked to people who did not vote, who took the process and democracy for granted. After Trump, I got angry, and I believe that people around the country got angry with me. In America, we typically have low voter turnout and engagement with a few exceptions. In 2008, for example, according to the Pew Research Center, the levels of participation by eligible voters of color, particularly Black women, and younger voters, dramatically increased. It was a record year, not only because Black women, for the first time, had the highest voter turnout rate, but also, because for the first time since 1968, voter turnout was 61.6%.

Unfortunately, it started falling again, and by 2016, voter turnout was 55.7%. To put that in context, America ranked 30th out of 35 nations for voter turnout. Trump changed all of that as people quickly realized that democracy is fragile and that our society works because of accepted social norms and not just the rule of law. We always assumed that candidates would release their tax statements until Trump did not. We just assumed that presidents bought the country together until Trump did not. We just assumed that if there were a global outbreak, our president would work to keep us safe until Trump did not. We never thought our president would turn a blind eye to democracy, humanity, civility, and personal financial gain until Trump did. Trump, by many accounts, was an evil president, but I believe he was a necessary evil. He woke people up. Over the past four years, people of all ages have been more politically engaged, and we have witnessed more women and people of color get elected to office. And even though the Democratic Party ultimately selected Joe Biden to run for president, it was an incredibly diverse field of qualified candidates, and he chose a woman of color, Kamala Harris, as his running mate.

We have learned the hard way that elections have consequences, and that when we vote, there is more on the ballot than just who will be our next president. We are voting for the heart and soul of our nation. My Nana told me that when she voted, she was doing it for us, the   children of her children. This year, when I voted *against* Trump, I did the same.

2020: the year we went to hell

12/24/2020

2020 has changed us. It has broken us, transmogrified us, and challenged us. It has been a year where we have learned who we are and what we are willing to do to survive. There are days when I wake up, and I am so disappointed with my elected officials, fellow Americans, and myself. How have we allowed this to become our here and now? I used to laugh when people talked about making America great again, and now I find myself just wanting us to aspire to be mediocre. Greatness, at least in the near future, is no longer within our reach. Any country that would put a man in office and support him as he lied, obfuscated, and deceived people and then watched as millions of them tested positive for COVID-19 and thousands of them died from it cannot lay claim to greatness again. America is tragically flawed because of our long history of classism and racism, because of White supremacy and White privilege, and because we dare to ask God to bless us while we curse one another.

In 1967, in a speech to The Hungry Club Forum in Atlanta, Dr. King talked about how America was wrestling with three major evils: the evils of racism, the evil of poverty, and the evil of war. He urged us to confront these evils and dismantle them. He said we must continue to fight to keep the pressure on until America changes. One year later, in Memphis, Tennessee, one day before he would be assassinated, Dr. King sent ahead the title of his Sunday sermon, "Why America May Go to Hell." Fifty-two years later, I believe that the dark days that Dr. King had tried to warn us about have finally come to pass. 2020 has been the year, under this president, while we are in a global pandemic and national, racial awakening, that America has gone to hell. We are in the Ninth Circle, screaming and crying out for relief. We are watching as our elected officials—many of whom are millionaires, and all of whom are making more than three times the average salary—fail to get over themselves and their petty politics so that they can come together and provide us with some relief. Every country seems to be leaning in to help their citizens except us. We have received one stimulus check as an eviction crisis is happening, as small businesses are closing, as our children are being educated from our kitchen tables, as our positive case numbers are rising, and as incomes are falling. Our politicians are playing politics as millions of us struggle to pay our bills. I have never been so disgusted and frankly embarrassed to be an American.

My father says that there have been moments when he thought America was standing on the edge of the abyss, and he watched as it slowly redeemed itself. He believes that the swinging pendulum always finds a way to level off. "The bombing of the Sixteenth Street Baptist, the assassination of Dr. King, the 1968 riots, Reaganomics, the Three Strikes Rule," he slowly ticks through a list, "all moments when I thought we were not going to be able to come back, but we did because America, as racist and classist as she is, just keeps surviving." My father, I realized, is more hopeful than I am. Perhaps it is because he is a Baptist minister, or maybe it is because he has seen this country at its worst and was still able to pray for it to be better. I used to have a lot of hope for and in America. I believed that the moral arc of the universe, as Dr. King would say, was bending toward justice and that it was my responsibility to keep bending it until it got there. I thought it would get there and that justice was soon come. 2020 has shown me differently. I have watched the battle over mask-wearing, the voter suppression tactics, the killing of Black men and women, the blatant disregard for our pain and suffering, and I am not convinced that we are moving toward anything better.

I recognize that we are in the last days of the Trump era, but the damage that he and his supporters have done to the soul of our nation will not be healed for years to come. President-elect Joe Biden and Madame Vice-President-elect Kamala Harris will spend the next four years trying to get us out of this abyss, trying to stop the bleeding, trying to end the suffering, trying to get us out of hell. 2020 has been that year: the one that nightmares and scary movies are made of, the one that feels like it will never end. Dr. King said there are times when you must take a stand simply because it is right. It may not be political or safe or popular, but it is the one that is right. In this moment, as I look out across the landscape of America, the only thing that feels right is deciding to survive, to get up, throw my shoulders back, put on my face-mask, lean into the wind that is sure to come, and just survive. After 11 months of COVID-19, four years of Donald Trump, and 401 years of racism and White supremacy, making the decision to survive the best that I can do at this moment.

2020: a year that tried but failed to break us

12/31/2020

There are moments in your life that are so overwhelming that they take your breath away. Moments that when you look back, you remember every detail like it just happened. My mother remembers the day that Dr. King was assassinated. She had just made dinner and was feeling hot and exhausted. She was six months pregnant, and since we did not have central air, my mother was sitting out on the front porch drinking a glass of my Nana's lemonade and eating a small slice of pound cake. She remembers that lemonade was sour and that she was contemplating getting up and adding more sugar. She was moving a little slowly because her ankles had swollen, and she wondered if it had anything to do with the fatback she had eaten for dinner the night before. It had been, she said, a beautiful day. Quiet and still. My father was sitting in the living room, listening to the radio. He had come home a little early because they were planning to attend choir practice. She heard my father scream, and she jumped up, faster than she thought she could move and ran inside. She said her heart was beating so loudly she could hear it. My father was crying and pacing the floor, and when he told her, she said that time stood still, and she could not breathe. I remember 9-11 the same way: the sounds, the smells, the temperature. I remember what I was wearing, what I ate that morning for breakfast, and what I was thinking about on the subway while I made my way to work. I remember watching that second plane hit, out the corner of my eye, and having to sit down because I could not catch my breath. These are moments that stand still, that live in infamy, that forever define who you are and how you see the world.

2020 has been that kind of year, filled with so many of those moments. It has haunted us, kept us up at night, and made us question who we are and who we want to be as citizens of this country. When Dr. King was assassinated, the world stood still and mourned. We stopped to remember what happened at Gettysburg or on D-Day. We stopped for three days after 9-11 happened so we could catch our breath, we could say their names, we could remember. We came together and mourned as a nation because we knew that it was through the collective mourning that we are reminded that we are stronger than our struggles. We have lost more Americans due to COVID-19 in one year than we did during World War II. On average, we have lost 975 Americans per day. And yet, we have not stopped. We have not collectively mourned. To date, 19.4 million Americans have tested positive for COVID, and 335,000+ Americans have died. We are in a war against this novel coronavirus, and we are losing.

If you are Black in America, you are fighting not just one war but two: against COVID and against racism because even though Black people make up only 13.1 % of the population, we comprise 17% of the COVID deaths. Black people have died at 3.6 times the rate of White people. Black women are more likely to get COVID, and Black men are more likely to die from it. The data does not surprise us, we know that when White folks catch a cold, we catch pneumonia, and when White folks catch and survive

COVID, we die from it. When children test positive for COVID, White children will survive it while Black (and Brown) children die from it. Racism has caused the conditions that have led us here: Black people have a 60 percent higher rate of diabetes and a 40 percent higher rate of hypertension; we are less likely to receive adequate health care; and more likely to work jobs that keep us on the frontline. We tend to live in food deserts and fast-food swamps, and even when we show up at the hospital, as doctors or lawyers or teachers—as learned and credentialed individuals—we are not given the highest level of treatment and care. According to Dr. Susan Moore, a Black woman physician who was denied adequate care while she struggled with COVID and later died of complications from it, this is how Black people get killed because we are sent home, and we do not know how to fight for ourselves.

In *Their Eyes Were Watching God*, Zora Neale Hurston wrote that there are years that ask questions and years that answer. For Black people, 2020 has done both as Black Lives Matter met Black COVID-19 Stories. George Floyd. Breonna Taylor. Ahmaud Arbery. This year has exposed how deeply divided our country is and how and why America's experiment with democracy has failed. It forced us to ask questions about our future in this country and demanded that we brainstorm solutions to ensure our survival. Skylar Herbert. Antwion Ball. Shirley and Demetria Bannister. Susan Moore. 2020 exposed the roots of some White folks' racism and hatred of us, and it laid bare our collective pain and our wounds. This is a year that will define us, but it will not break us. We have survived too much and have come too far. We will be the ones to restore the glory, to find the moments of joy, and have hope and faith. We will find ways to laugh through the tears and pray through our pain as we look forward to the morning and to what is coming next. I look forward to being there with you and getting to the other side of this War together. Àṣẹ.

2021: it is (past) time for y'all to be anti-racist

1/22/2021

Now that we are at the end of Donald Trump's reign and we can feel the collective temperature of our nation begin to drop, we should probably take a moment to look back at what we have learned before the Whitewashing of history begins. It is becoming increasingly apparent that every conversation in Trump's America was about race, even when it was not. It is simply because every conversation about race in this country was (and is) a conversation about people in this country. Race is not a biological concept; it is a social construct that either extends or denies a person's access to privileges and benefits. Conversations about race are messy and emotional, unsettling, and frightening and where you stand on the question of race is an easy barometer to finding out where you stand on just about everything else.

I was seven years old when I had my first conversation about race. Growing up, I was raised between my parents' home in Washington, DC, and my grandparents' homes in South Carolina. My parents would drop me off, and I would spend the entire summer moving between my Nana's middle-class home in Columbia and my grandmother's dirt-floor farm in Lexington. Both places answered questions in my soul that I did not know that I had. There was something to be said about running around my grandmother's land, which had a barn full of animals, trees, a lake, and where the only neighbors were family. In contrast, my Nana's house was in the city, and my best friend was a little White boy who lived four houses down on the right. As soon as I got out of the car, before I unpacked my bag or changed my clothes, I would run down to his house to let him know that I was back, and we could play. I remember that summer and that day when he was upset, kicking rocks, with his hands in his pockets. He said his Daddy was angry about those "Yankee n-words," always coming down from the North, acting uppity, and trying to take over. His Daddy said the South was going to rise again and put those "Yankee n-words" in their place. My friend said he hated them and wanted them dead. And I said, me too! When I told my Nana later that evening, two things happened: that was my first conversation about race and my last time playing with him. Over time, I learned that conversations about race are just conversations about people and about bigotry and who has the inalienable right to life, liberty, property, and the pursuit of happiness. It is about who has access and who does not.

America is tragically flawed because our foundation is built upon the oppression and servitude of Black people. It is built upon racism, the parent of race, which means that it is woven into every facet of our lives from the womb to the grave. It shows up in the mass industrial prison complex, in our schools, in the redlining of mortgages by banks in our communities, through voter suppression, racial profiling, and racist police practices. It is the backbone of our economy and even shows up in our medical field, where Black people are more likely to die first and die more.

Conversations about race are not about race; they are about people, and the only way to change the conversation is to confront it, address it, and challenge it. In a racist society, Angela Davis said it is not enough to be non-racist; we must be *anti-racist*. Ibram Kendi, picking up on this idea, wrote that to be anti-racist, you must first learn what racism is and how it has evolved. You need to study the history to understand how race works in America. Once you do that, you then need to figure out where you sit with the question of race: Who are you? How do you define yourself? Where are you in your racial identity awareness? You must be honest with yourself and become painfully aware of your own racist beliefs and stereotypes. You must be prepared to do the hard work to change and to confront others to change as well. You need to be bold in confronting racism, you must speak up, seek it out and then call it out. You cannot be quietly anti-racist.

We have the advantage of the long eye of racial American history, and we know that racism was written into our Constitution by the so-called founding fathers, and it has been codified into law. We know that racism has ramifications and that it is an old seed that was planted, watered, and nurtured. It is embedded into the foundation of our country. Anti-racist work is the ax that we take to the root. What we know and what we have learned in Trump's America is that we are the hunters, and either we are swinging that ax to the root, or we are swinging at others to keep them away from it. In Trump's America, it was easy for people to talk about doing the hard work; in Joe Biden and Kamala Harris's America, say less and do more. Every conversation in this country is a conversation about race because it is a conversation about people. Your job now is to change the conversation, answer the most persistent questions, and challenge yourselves and everyone around you to be anti-racist.

Abolish the damn police

5/11/2021

Like many of you, I counted down the moments, with both trep-idation and worry, to the reading of the verdict in the Derek Chauvin trial. As someone who has both studied and witnessed state-sanctioned violence against the Black community and who grew listening to my father talk about how the brutal murder of Emmett Till instilled a deep-rooted fear of White men in young Black boys throughout the South—I do not have much faith in a system that is rooted in White supremacy. As I watched Chauvin's face as the verdict was read, his look of surprise, in many ways, mirrored my own. Given that less than 5% of police officers who commit unspeakable acts of atrocity against our communities are held responsible, I was not expecting the system to work the way it was supposed to. I watched as people cheered and cried, exhaled and hugged, and I could not help but wonder what our lives would be like if police accountability for the killing of unarmed Black and Brown people was the norm and not the rare exception. I sat there after hearing the verdict, and though I wanted to exhale, I knew that I could not because this was only a small step toward moving us closer to where we need to be so that we can be safe in this country. I was reminded of something that Angela Davis once said, after the failure of the grand jury to indict Darren Wilson for the murder of Michael Brown: "There is so much history of this racist violence that simply to bring one person to justice is not going to disturb the whole racist edifice."

This past year has been challenging for the Black and Brown communities as we have struggled with both the devasting impact of COVID-19 and the increased reality that we are still fighting to convince the world that our lives matter. We are in the middle of a syndemic, fighting to breathe, fighting to survive, and fighting to find moments of peace and joy. According to Mapping Police Violence, the reality is that more than 1,000 unarmed people died due to police harm between 2013 and 2019, and about a third of them were Black. Additionally, about 17% of the Black people who died due to police harm were unarmed, a larger share than any other racial group and almost a third more than the average of 13%. In 2020, between January and August, police killed at least one Black person every week, and only two states, Rhode Island, and Vermont, reported no police killings of Black people.

During the trial of Derek Chauvin, approximately 75 people have been killed by the police, including 20-year-old Daunte Wright, 13-year-old Adam Toledo, and 16-year-old Ma'Khia Bryant. Since the reading of the verdict, Andrew Brown, Jr. was shot and killed, and Isaiah Brown was shot at least ten times (he is currently in critical condition). In every case, there was a rush by the police and the media to shape the narrative, to criminalize the victim, and to spin a story that would justify why a routine encounter with the police would once again end with a funeral, a cry for justice, and push to forgive and move on.

The American policing system, which has its roots in slave patrols and Jim Crow, is not broken. It is racist and built on White supremacy and Whiteness. It is unfair. It is deeply problematic. It is designed to terrorize us and force us to submit. It is all of this and so much more, but it is not broken because it does precisely what it was designed to do. We cannot fix this system; we must break it and then build back something better. We must begin to imagine a world without police brutality and where Black and Brown people are treated with justice and equity and then work like hell to make it happen.

This is the moment when we must fight. This is the moment when we must stand. This is the moment when we must hold fast to our dreams for what this country can and should become. We add our voice to the growing chorus of organizations and individuals speaking out in support of the Chauvin verdict, but we are clear that this is not the end of our work but just (yet another) beginning. We know that pain and joy can exist in the same space. We invite you to stop and hold space with us for all the families who have not received justice but who are, at this moment, finding some peace and perhaps some joy. "Freedom," as Coretta Scott King reminded us, "is never really won. You earn it and win it in every generation." We do that by standing together, fighting together, dreaming together, mourning, and grieving together, and working to dismantle a White supremacist system together.

Blood on the leaves and blood at the roots

6/26/2020

Southern trees, Billie Holiday once sang, bear strange fruit, and when this happens, blood is on the leaves and blood is at the roots. Everything should close when an unarmed Black person gets killed in this country. All movements, in all communities, should come to a standstill so that we can have a day to grieve, a moment to mourn. We should dress in White, head down to the river, pour some libations, and say their names: Breonna Taylor, Ahmaud Arbery, George Floyd. We should burn some incense, light some sage, and then do to White supremacy what White folks did to Black Wall Street and Rosewood. We should use the long eye of history, read *Black Power: The Politics of Liberation*, and realize that within a racist and capitalist society, power never concedes or relents or gives in without a struggle, without a war. Coretta Scott King, whose husband was hated and feared by the parents of the adults who now revere his name, once said that freedom is never really won because you must earn it and win it in every generation. And Malcolm X, who was murdered in cold blood in front of his family, once proclaimed that if you are not ready to die for freedom, remove the word from your vocabulary.

Medgar Evers, who was shot and killed in his own driveway, noted that freedom has never been free. We should have a day to mourn when they kill us and use it as a time to remind ourselves that freedom, if that is what we are genuinely seeking, will cost us everything we have. We should say the names of those that have been killed—Botham Jean, Atatiana Jefferson, Rayshard Brooks—lift them up and then proceed to act as decisively as this country acts when Whiteness, militarized and authorized, fights against us.

In 1967, at the height of the Vietnam War, Dr. King, the Nobel Peace Prize winner, and one-time darling of the Civil Rights Movement, radically changed his tactics. He was no longer talking about the dream of integration but the nightmare of American capitalism, racism, and militarism. Dr. King was no longer talking about holding hands and singing freedom songs; instead, he was actively pursuing an aggressive political, antiwar, and socioeconomic agenda. He was relentless and unflinching in his call for a $50 billion-dollar massive federal aid program for Black people. They killed him, not because he was calling for little Black boys and girls to hold hands with little White boys and girls but because he was challenging American imperialism and calling for them to dismantle capitalism. America is an evil and greedy country, and Black economic independence is a threat to the White-dominated capitalism that grips this country, oppresses us, and kills us with impunity.

In 1921, during the Tulsa race massacre and in 1923 in Rosewood, White people killed, destroyed, looted, and burned Black neighborhoods to the ground. It was an act of domestic terror designed to silence us and break us. Every time we rise, White people organize to beat us back down. In 1865, with the ratification of the 13th Amendment, there was a push to provide some form of reparations: 40 acres, a mule, and 50 dollars.

There was probably some excitement and a whole lot of trepidation because after seeing the evilness of White people up close, formerly enslaved people understood that power never concedes without a battle plan to attack. It never has, and it never will. Six days later, secret White societies, including the Ku Klux Klan and the White Brotherhood, were founded to restore White order and rule back to the South. They were trying to break us, to scare us into submission. They terrorized us, burned crosses on our property, kidnapped, raped, beat, and lynched us. They were brutal in their efficiency, holding cookouts with their wives and children, while Black bodies, a strange and bitter crop, were hanging from the trees. According to the Equal Justice Initiative, between Reconstruction and World War II, more than 4,400 racial terror lynchings happened in this country. Lynching is a particular form of targeted domestic terrorism designed to remind us to hold our peace, remember our place, not fight back.

Since May 27th, amid the most massive movement for Black lives, six people of color—a woman, four men and a teenage boy—have been found hanging from a tree. Officials say that the investigations so far point to suicide, but in our hearts, in our spirits, we know that we have been here before. Everything should close when Black and Brown bodies are found swinging in the breeze. We need a day to grieve and a moment to mourn. We should dress in White, head down to the river, pour some libations, and say the names that we know: Otis "Titi" Gulley, Robert Fuller, Malcolm Harsch, Dominique Alexander. We mourn, and then we fight back with the same type of ruthlessness and arrogance that led enslavers to demand freedom from the British while simultaneously enslaving us. We fight back until the killing of Black boys and Black girls—to paraphrase Ella Baker—is as important as the killing of White boys and White girls. We fight for freedom until it is won.

We are a long-memoried people

5/17/2020

As a little girl, whenever something happened to me, my Nana would tell me to write it down, to record it, to get my stories on paper. She said that we are a long-memoried people, and we document our pain so that the children of our children will know that they are the descendants of people who know how to survive. We speak our truth into the wind so that we can force this country to bear witness, to not look away. During the 1850s, abolitionist William Still recorded the names and stories of hundreds of escaped enslaved people who were fleeing to freedom on the Underground Railroad. Between 1920-1938, the National Association for the Advancement of Colored People (NAACP) hung a flag out the window of their Manhattan office that read, "A man was lynched yesterday." In 1968, my Nana, who was a nurse, taped a sign to her hospital locker that said, "Black people are dying today so we can be free tomorrow." In 2015, the African American Policy Forum, led by Kimberlé Crenshaw, launched the #SayHerName campaign to document the names and stories of Black women and girls who had died at the hands of racist police violence. We tell our stories. We record our pain.

At the beginning of March, I launched #BlackCovidStories to record and remember and recognize our pain. COVID-19 is devasting our community, and nationwide, we are dying at double the rate of our state population. We are standing at the center of America's viral, racial, and economic epidemic. When the virus began to rapidly spread across the globe and Trump chose a wait-and-see approach, I knew then that our communities, once hit, would be devasted. We live in a country where Black men have the lowest life expectancy, dying four years earlier than White men, seven years earlier than Black women, and, nine years earlier than White women. Black women, who are three to four times more likely to die from pregnancy-related causes than White women, have the worst maternal mortality rate of any industrialized country. In 2019, Black men and boys were 2.5 times more likely than White men and boys to die during an encounter with the police. We have the highest poverty rates, the highest unemployment numbers, and we disproportionately suffer from the underlying health conditions such as diabetes mellitus, chronic lung disease, and cardiovascular disease that led to the most severe cases of COVID-19.

When America began to act to slow the spread of the virus, schools were closed, and people were told to work from home. In our community, less than 20 percent or one out of five Black workers can work from home. We were quickly reclassified as essential, but what that meant, for many of us, was that we were expendable. We are a long-memoried people, and we know what it means and how it feels when White America offers our bodies up for sacrifice. Even though Black people are 13 percent of the population, we represent 30 percent of the bus drivers and about 20 percent of all food service workers, janitors, cashiers, and store stockers. We do not have the luxury to stay at home, and we are experiencing the impact of this reality on our communities.

Black women are more likely to test positive for it, and Black men are more likely to die from it.

We are the descendants of men and women who chose to survive, and who did it by gathering together. In moments of grief, Black people gathered. In moments of sorrow, we gathered. In moments of frustration and pain, terror and fear, we gathered. We gathered together during slavery, meeting in the woods to pray and learn. We gathered during Reconstruction, holding classes in our church basements to learn how to read. We gathered during Jim Crow, meeting in our club rooms to get built back up. We gathered during the Civil Rights Movement, meeting in our homes to plan, to prepare, to get motivated and be inspired. We gathered during times of crisis from Reaganomics to Black Lives Matter, to the night of Donald Trump's election, so that we could be together, support, love and lean on one another. Black people, we gather. It is how we find strength, how we shoulder each other's burden and how we love each other. We are in a moment of crisis yet again, when White America is getting and surviving COVID-19 while we are getting and dying from it.

We are a long-memoried people, and we know that because of what we have been through in this country, we are survivors, we are magic, we are brilliant, and we are geniuses; but what we are not is immune to COVID-19. At the beginning of March, I had a long conversation with my father, trying to explain why he needed to adopt a different tactical plan if he wanted to beat this virus. My daddy is a fighter. He is a Vietnam War-era veteran, Civil Rights Movement activist, bishop, and pastor. He grew up in Jim Crow South Carolina, where he learned early on how to dodge racial bullets, and how to stay alive amid extreme Whiteness. He is not, as he clearly stated to me, afraid of the coronavirus; but my father has diabetes and high blood pressure. He is a prostate cancer survivor and had quadruple bypass heart surgery. I told him that he needed a new survival plan because beating COVID is not about being brave; it is about being smart. We must be smart now so that we can gather together later, so we can one day speak their names, and lean on and love on one another. We are a strong-willed and stubborn people, and since we have survived so much for so long, we will keep rising, we will keep going forward, and we will survive what is happening on this planet, in this country, right now.

Dead men walking

3/12/2020

A few days ago, a young Black man was killed in this city. I do not know which block or which neighborhood, but I do know that it happened because it always happens. These are the times that try our collective soul. We need some air. We need to breathe. We need a moment to exhale, regroup, take stock. Between the Mayoral election (which feels like recycled air), the rising homicide numbers, and the ever-growing threat of COVID-19, we just need a moment. Everything is happening at once in the city, and it feels overwhelming. I have spent the past two weeks planning for the inevitable, driving around the city collecting supplies and stories. I am a storyteller, and two years ago, I committed myself to telling our Baltimore stories. When I was growing up, my mother said to me that I was a natural-born writer and a storyteller. She gave me my first journal when I was 13 years old and told me to write and record our stories. "I am starting to believe that this world doesn't want Black people to survive," she'd say, "so your job is to record our stories so that even if we are not here, our words are, our lives are. You must write to make sure we are not forgotten." So, I did. I started listening to my people and recording what I heard. It is second nature for me to lean in and listen.

This is why I love Baltimore and why it breaks my heart. We are a city with a million stories, and yet we are told that only a few voices matter. We have become used to corruption and violence, being lied to by our politicians and mistreated by those in leadership. We have borne witness to thousands of lives being lost or tragically altered in this city due to violence and corruption. It is not uncommon to see people gather at the spots where a life was lost or to smell the burning sage as we try to find peace within our moments of tragedy. At the end of 2019, Baltimore City recorded 348 people who had died due to homicide, and over 1,000 people had been involved in a non-fatal shooting.

We are almost in the middle of March, only 55 days into 2020, and we have already had 54 homicides (as of March 10). I am convinced that there is a way forward. However, I am just not convinced that everyone in this city is ready to move in that direction. Our death and our suffering are as much a part of this city as political corruption and economic inequality. I have spent time walking through the city visiting stores and trying to get a sense of how people are prepping for the looming coronavirus pandemic. It is during these moments when I am reminded that preparing for a disaster that you cannot see and have never experienced is a luxury. It is a privilege to be able to purchase one month's worth of food, medicines, and supplies. The assumption is that you have savings that you can tap into, or that you have money that you can move around, and, you have the security of knowing that even if you must stay home, you will still get paid. Disaster planning is not for the faint of heart or the poor.

I spent last week visiting Edmondson Village, purchasing toilet paper and cough medicine. I met Valerie, an elderly Black woman, who was not as worried about the coronavirus as she was about the violence in the community. "I got robbed last week," she began, "and I'm an old woman. Why would they think that I had money?" She was sweating a little bit and was leaning on the counter. My heart broke as she spoke about watching the boys in her neighborhood go from sitting on the stoop to standing on the corner. "I always watch them and talk to them, and sometimes I can see when their dreams disappear." She kept talking but I stayed right there, at that moment, trying to imagine what it looked like when your dreams disappeared. She said that you can see the light of possibility go out in their eyes and get replaced with a look of desperate hunger, greed, a touch of anger. "It is actually frightening to see it happen." She kept talking and I kept listening. I took notes, and she wanted to know why. "I'm nobody special," she laughed. "I'm just like everybody else. We all have a story to tell about our life in this city."

We talked about the coronavirus and homicides: "I'm tired of our kids' shooting and killing each other. We need to put somebody in office who cares that we are dying. We need them to turn that light back on in the eyes of our children." I helped her put her groceries in the cart and I walked out with her. I offered her a ride, but she wanted to walk. She grabbed my hand before she left, and she reminded me so much of my Nana that I had to stop myself from hugging her. "A young boy got killed around here last week. You should write about him," she paused for a moment and sighed. "Black boys are always getting killed somewhere in this city. They're dead men walking; they just don't know it yet. Write about them; tell their stories."

Slavery and Whiteness
tried to erase us
8/17/2020

Do you know who you are? This is a question that has kept me up at night for the past 13 years. When my son was six, his independent and predominantly White school did a play about Thanksgiving. They sang songs about Columbus's greatness, the gratitude of the Native Americans, and the surprising discovery and taming of America. As I sat there watching my son participate in an ongoing narrative based and rooted in lies and the erasure of Indigenous people, I experienced a moment of cognitive dissonance. I became acutely aware that my son was the only Black boy on that stage.

I probably should have pulled him from the school; instead, I told myself that it was not the 1950s and that he was not Ruby Bridges or Little Rock Nine. I told myself that we did not live in Alabama or Mississippi, nor did he have to walk through crowds of angry White people to get into the school. Despite what my civil rights activist father had taught me, I believed that equality and justice had arrived. I remember sitting there, clapping, and feeling like a fraud. I looked around at the other moms who were wiping tears of joy while breathlessly commenting on how our children were brilliant and talented. During the reception, one of the White moms told her son that their family line traced back to the Mayflower and that when they got home, she would show him the family tree, so that he could know who he was. As I rolled my eyes and began to pack my bags to leave, my son turned to ask me whether our family came on the Mayflower too. He was sincere and wanted to know our family's history. Standing at that school, in the middle of the Founder's Library, drinking tea and eating finger sandwiches, I did not know how to tell him that I did not know.

I did not know how to say that slavery and Whiteness had stolen almost everything from us, especially our names and historical legacy. I did not know how to properly articulate that our people were considered property and were typically listed by gender and not name. I did not know how to tell him that we were the descendants of enslaved people, and that play, where he had spent days practicing and learning the songs and his lines, was a deliberate and intentional erasure and denial of us. I could not say that our people had been enslaved in South Carolina, the first state to secede from the Union, a place where Black bodies were bridges of entitlement for White families to stand on. I could not say any of this, so I said that we came from people who chose to survive. I want to say that I woke up at that moment and committed myself to challenge the lies and speak the truth, but that is not what happened. I spent the next few years trying to negotiate Whiteness while sending my sons into the belly of the beast of Whiteness every day. It took some time before I could admit that America is rooted in White supremacy and White nationalism and then to commit myself to dismantling it. I realized that sending my sons to predominantly White schools and then not working to bring in more families of color helped perpetuate inequity. I was so focused on my sons' success that I had become an opportunity hoarder, supporting a system that purposely miseducated so many of our children. I failed my son that day by not telling him the truth, but I became determined not to fail the children of my children. I became committed to researching our stories and reclaiming our names.

It took 13 years of research and working with our family's unofficial genealogists before I could sit down with my sons and tell them that I know who they are, and I know who I am. I showed them our family tree and then said, this is your grandmother's line; this is who you are. You are the sons of Karsonya and Johnnie and the grandsons of Bonnie Ruth Nix and Carson Eugene Wise Sr., the great-grandsons of Dorothy Mae Best Griffith and James Bamberg, the 2nd-great-grandsons of Lumisher Best and Hugo Griffith, and the 3rd-great-grandsons of Bannah Dora and Moses Best. You are the 4th-great-grandnephews of Fannie Robinson and Sammy Dickerson, which is the last generation of our family to be born enslaved. You are the 5th-great-grandsons of Moses Roberson; and the 6th-great-grandsons of Mary and Zed Roberson. They were speechless when I finished saying their names because they understood the significance of this moment. They know that slavery and Whiteness tried to erase us. They know that the policies, practices, and laws of that time were meant to discard us, dehumanize us, break us, consume, and control us. They were designed to bury us and to own us forever. But our family, our ancestors, chose to survive. I started researching our history based on a question from my six-year-old son, and I am grateful that at 19, he finally received his answer.

Do you know who you are? For Black people, this is a question that we must answer, not for ourselves but for our children. They must understand that our ancestors were more than property, more than bridges; they were survivors, and they chose to survive for us.

White men are "They the people"

10/16/2020

When I was 13 years old, my teacher made us memorize the Preamble to the Constitution. I used to read it every night, and early on, I believed that the words and the sentiment applied to everyone. *I Was The People.* My father, a Vietnam veteran, and Civil Rights Movement activist told me that Black people were the invisible hand that set this country's moral compass. If America, he said, was ever going to be the America that the White founding fathers wrote about, then it was up to us. He talked about the three branches of government and why he believed that the most vital branch, the one that got the least attention but was directly responsible for how we lived, was the judicial branch.

In his opinion, the real power was not to enforce the laws or even make the laws but to interpret them. It's the grey area, he explained, that determines district lines or school integration. It is the interpretation that shapes Miranda rights or strengthens or weakens the 13th Amendment. He would point at me and then at himself and say, "*We Are The People*," not them. It is our job to remind them. He would often cite the 58 years between the 1896 *Plessy v. Ferguson* case that upheld the constitutionality of racial segregation and the 1954 *Brown v. Board* case that ruled that racial segregation was unconstitutional as an example of how long it takes for the Supreme Court to "overrule" itself. He would hit the dashboard and say that people failed to understand how the court's interpretation of the law directly shapes this country. Thurgood Marshall knew this, he said, not only because he was on the legal team that challenged *Plessy* but because he lived through it and consciously chose to use his own experiences as a lens through which to see and interpret the law.

During the 1991 confirmation hearings for Clarence Thomas, my father and I spoke on the phone every night. He was furious that the Republican Party was using their political advantage to fill the Marshall seat with a Justice who was Black but who was not using his own experiences to influence how he interpreted the law. I could hear the frustration and anger and fear in his voice. All my skinfolk, as Zora Neale Hurston once wrote, ain't kinfolk. My father was right to be worried as Thomas has spent the last 28 years on the Supreme Court and is now the court's most conservative justice. My father believes that our nation's heart and soul's battleground is the courtroom, not the streets or the schools or the churches. This year the Supreme Court will decide on the Affordable Care Act, elections, religious rights, technology, the Mueller investigation and quite possibly the 2020 election, to name just a few.

Like my father, Donald Trump and the Republican Party understand where the battle is happening as Trump has already successfully appointed over 200 federal judges to lifetime appointments. This record is remarkable as Trump has appointed almost a quarter of all active federal judges in the United States. By contrast, in eight years, Barack Obama appointed 312 of the currently active federal judges, George W. Bush appointed 166, and Bill Clinton appointed 87. What is even more striking about his record is that Trump has appointed 53 appeals court judges, a powerful position as they are the regional gatekeepers who provide the final word on most appeals that do not end up in the Supreme Court. Even though Trump has appointed more women than other recent Republican presidents (he has appointed 48), 85 percent of all his appointed jurists are White. So, if the battleground is indeed the courtroom, then the people who are determining this nation's heart and soul are still over-whelmingly White, male, and conservative. As we watched his tweets and complained about his erratic, maniacal behavior, Trump, with the help of the Republican-led Senate, has quietly transformed *We The People* back into *They The People*.

America is not the greatest country in the world

6/6/2022

We are short-memoried people. We move quickly from one tragedy to the next, and despite our best intentions, it has become much harder to focus on and try to fix one thing because there is just too much happening. There is too much grief. There is too much sorrow. It is exhausting because there have been too many bodies, bullets, marches, vigils, candles, and hashtags to mourn appropriately. We have learned how to bury our pain and build monuments over our ruins. I do not believe that the human spirit is equipped to handle the amount of collective pain we are dealing with at this moment.

In the last month, we have marked one million people who have died from COVID-19, and there has been a marked uptick in violent crime across the country including a White supremacist domestic terrorist who targeted and killed 10 Black people at a grocery store and a mass shooting at Robb Elementary School where 19 children and two teachers were killed. "To look around the United States today is enough to make prophets and angels weep," James Baldwin once wrote. Even with all this pain, school shootings should really hit differently and should lead to change. Children are our future, and they are the most vulnerable part of our society. In the Maasai culture, the traditional greeting is "Casserian Energi," which means "How are the children?" They believe that the best determinant for their community's future health and prosperity is the mental, emotional, and psychological well-being of their children. As I have asked countless times before, I ask now, "America, how are our children doing?" I believe that our children are not doing well because we are failing them.

There is a cycle of emotions from fear to sorrow to anger every time there is a school shooting in this country. We demand change, and for a few days, before we look away, we believe that change is coming.

And then nothing happens.

I remember Columbine and the fear and anger that everyone expressed in 1999. This was before social media, when we sent emails and made phone calls or marched to get our elected officials to do something. And nothing happened. I remember Sandy Hook in 2012 and how I believed that after the senseless murder of 20 children and six teachers, America would do what the United Kingdom did in 1996 after the Dunblane Massacre. On March 13, 1996, a gunman went into Dunblane Primary School and shot and killed 16 children and one teacher. In response to the outrage and petitions from the people, two firearms acts were passed, one of which outlawed the private ownership of most handguns within the U.K. The Dunblane Massacre was the deadliest school shooting in the U.K.—and the last. Here in America, after Sandy Hook, the cycle of emotions started, and when we finally looked away, nothing had changed. I am not convinced that gun laws will change in this country, even less than a month after America had one mass shooting per day for an entire week that ended with a mass shooting in Buffalo.

There comes a moment when you must accept the truth and what it says about you despite what you have been led to believe. We are not the greatest country in the world. This is not what greatness looks like, and it is not how greatness chooses to respond amid a troubling and overwhelming moment. If we were great and if we really loved our children, then attacks against them would lead to not only prayers, thoughts, and vigils but also change. We would move mountains to ensure that our children were safe.

We live in a country that has more guns than people. There are 258.3 million adults in America, and there are estimated to be over 400 million guns among the police, the military, and civilians, with civilians owning 393 million. According to the Pew Research Center, only 30 percent of Americans own a legally registered gun, so 98 percent of the registered guns in this country are in the hands of approximately 77 million people. The US has just 4 percent of the world's population but owns about 40 percent of civilian-owned guns globally. In this country, we are more likely to die from gun violence than from many leading causes of death combined. So far this year, there have been 212 mass shootings and 27 school shootings with injuries or deaths. In comparison, there were 693 in 2021, another 611 in 2020, and 417 in 2019. In 2019, after someone pointed a rifle at my youngest son and me, I reached out to a therapist friend who told me that when I feel most afraid, I should say to myself things like, "I am safe. My son is safe. We are safe." I have come back to this moment and said those words countless times, and every time I do, the realist in me whispers, "for now." I know that things will not change until Congress changes them.

According to the Sandy Hook Promise Foundation, they can start by passing both the Keep Americans Safe Act (H.R. 2510/S. 1108), which would prohibit the sale and transfer of high-capacity magazines, and the Assault Weapons Ban of 2021, which would ban the sale, transfer, manufacture, and importation of military-style assault weapons and high-capacity ammunition magazines. We also need to get rid of our obsession with guns because until we do that, we will never be safe. More importantly, our children will never be safe.

Black bodies have always mattered

2/24/2022

There is a place between who we want to be and who we are. It is a difficult, sobering place because it forces you to look at what you have done and then challenges you to do better. This is that moment, and, unfortunately, we have been here before. The end of the proclaimed Black History Month is that moment. America should have spent that last month deep diving into our history, our struggles, our stories. We should have been doing the same. This is the moment to scream that Black Lives Matter, even if what we see around us are constant reminders that they do not. We live in our country where Black bodies have always been valued even though they told us that Black lives did not matter. What we know to be true and what we should be teaching our children is that our History is THE History. It is through our tears, our sweat, our blood, our sacrifice, our struggle, our faith, our love, our laughter, our music, and our humanity that you can trace the American Story. Langston Hughes, in his poem, *Let America Be America Again*, wrote—I am the poor White, fooled and pushed apart/I am the Negro bearing slavery's scars./I am the Red man driven from the land,/I am the immigrant clutching the hope I seek..../O, yes,/I say it plain,/America never was America to me,/And yet I swear this oath--/America will be!

His vision of and for America is my vision as well. No matter how long it takes or what needs to be sacrificed along the way, America will be America for us. This is the moment, and like Angela Davis once said, we must "sink deep into the moment, husbanding this delight, hoarding it" because it will be short-lived. And even though we know how many of us have died for this American dream, we must walk into this moment confident and unafraid because somewhere buried deep in our genes is the familiarity of freedom. We know what it feels like, even though we are not experiencing it right now. We are the descendants of those who chose to survive.

In August 1619, when the first "20 and odd Negroes" arrived in Jamestown, VA, they did not know what their future held, but they did know their past. They remembered freedom and family; they remembered being loved and being valued. They remembered that their lives, their survival, and their sanity mattered. They understood that they were not the embodiment of evil and violence in this story; they were heroes or sheroes. They were not the footnote to the beginning of America's story; they were the story. They were the dawn of a new day. They were the hope and the dreams of their parents. They were survivors, and even if their story was not going to be written, it was going to survive. Their story showed up in my great-grandmother's eyes and my Nana's hands. It showed up in the laughter of my sons and in their quiet moments of resistance. They understood their worth and their value. Black bodies have always been valued in this country.

It was during this period, that the notions of race and slavery, as explained by historian Ira Berlin, were constantly being reevaluated. America moved from being a "nation with slaves" (where slavery was one of the economic pillars of the economy) to a "slave nation" (where slavery was the center of the economy). Our nation was built by Black hands on the backs of Black people and is being held together by the heart and soul of our collective Black humanity. It was built on the compromises that White men made about slavery, which was essentially about the worth and value of our people. According to economist Robert Evans, the slave market for the antebellum South was similar to the New York Stock Exchange because it "served in the eyes of the public as a sensitive reflector of current and future business prospects." So the market itself was driven by the cost and value of Black bodies. In 1860, an enslaved man, in good health and condition, was worth about $1,500, and an enslaved woman (essentially an enslaved girl of childbearing age) was worth about $1,325. Now to do the math for a moment: $1 in 1860 is worth $33.87 today, so an enslaved man, using today's money market, was worth about $50,805, and an enslaved woman, $44,877. Black bodies have always been valued even though we are told that our Black lives do not matter while showing us that our Black dollars do.

In 2019, according to the Selig Center for Economic Growth, Black buying power was $1.4 trillion, which is higher than the gross domestic product of Mexico. It is projected to grow to $1.8 trillion by 2024. At the same time, we have the lowest rates in homeownership, life insurance, college savings plans, and retirement accounts. We are outpaced in our wages by our White and Asian counterparts with the same skills and experience.

Black history month, which is supposed to be a time of reflection on what we have been through and pride for what we have overcome, has been transformed into a capitalist hodgepodge of *I Have a Dream Mattress Sales*, and *We Shall Overcome Designer Tennis Shoes*. It is designed to confuse us instead of giving us the clarity that we need to understand that we are descendants of survivors, and we are because they were. So as we move out of this month, let us do so knowing and proclaiming that Black history is American history and that without our story, there is no story to tell.

Justice is coming, but it ain't here yet

1/15/2022

In 1959, in a Commencement Address at Morehouse College, Dr. Martin Luther King Jr. told the graduating class that the great challenge facing them was to remain awake, alert, and creative through this great revolution. The country, according to Dr. King, was moving toward change, and if they continued to apply just the right amount of pressure, then there would be a "revolution in the social and political structure of our world on the question of the equality of man." This speech was only three years after the Montgomery Bus Boycott when there was a sense that the political and social protest campaign would change both the laws and the hearts and minds of people. In 1965, just a few years later, at a March in Selma, Alabama, Dr. King was asked, "How long will it take to see social justice?" He answered, "I come to say to you this afternoon, however difficult the moment, however frustrating the hour, it will not be long because truth crushed to earth will rise again. How long? Not long, because no lie can live forever. How long? Not long, because you shall reap what you sow. How long? Not long, because the arc of the moral universe is long, but it bends toward justice." (Now Dr. King was building on what Unitarian minister and abolitionist Theodore Parker wrote in 1853: "I do not pretend to understand the moral universe. The arc is a long one. My eye reaches but little ways. I cannot calculate the curve and complete the figure by the experience of sight. I can divide it by conscience. And from what I see, I am sure it bends toward justice.")

So for Dr. King, the work was about pushing this country, bending this country, moving this country toward justice. I sometimes wonder if the people who quote Dr. King today but who would not have supported him yesterday understand that justice is painful. Justice requires sacrifice. Justice means that something and someone has got to change. We are standing here at the crossroads of freedom and equality, an interesting time in American history because the arc that Dr. King and Theodore Parker talked about is still bending. Now, it may not be bending as quickly as I would like, but it is still bending. We have not yet gotten to that place where the valleys have been exalted, the hills and mountains have been made low, the rough places made plain, and every crooked place has been made straight. "The universe," as Dr. King once said, "is on the side of justice," but I believe that justice is taking a long time to get here. I am a product of the Jim Crow generation. I was raised by parents who survived one of the most tumultuous times in American history, the civil rights years. They remember where they were when a picture of Emmett Till's body was put on the cover of *Jet* magazine and what they were doing when they heard that Dr. King had been assassinated. They know that justice was never and will never be blind in this country, but like Dr. King and James Baldwin and Ida B. Wells and Mary McLeod Bethune and so many others they believe that *We, Too, Sing America*, and we can, and will reshape and save this nation.

My daddy once said that the problem with America is that

they quote Dr. King when it is expedient, but they do not study his words. In his words, Dr. King was a revolutionary because he fought against capitalism, the Vietnam War, and oppression. He advocated for unions, poverty eradication, and economic equality. Dr. King did not die for us to be free; a wicked and evil system worked together to assassinate him. We cannot ever let them forget that before Dr. King was assassinated, he was one of the most hated men in America, if not *the* most hated man. In 1968, his unfavorable numbers were 25 points higher than they had been in 1963 (when he wrote his Letter from a Birmingham Jail and when he spoke at the March on Washington for Jobs and Freedom). Dr. King also supported reparations. When Alex Haley interviewed him for *Playboy* magazine, Dr. King endorsed a $50 billion federal aid program for Black people that would, in his words, lead to "a spectacular decline" in "school dropouts, family breakups, crime rates, illegitimacy, swollen relief rolls, rioting and other social evils." He was fighting for us and against this system with every breath that he had.

So, how long will it take for justice to get here? I think that until we tell the truth about Dr. King's legacy, until we are honest about his words and his work, and until we are willing to take the same stand against the three evils that he did, justice will always be delayed and will always be denied.

#BlackCovidStories:
when tomorrow comes

5/8/2020

When my oldest son was born, my Nana told me that raising Black boys in America requires both courage and fearlessness. She said that I needed to learn how to move forward even when everything in me is telling me that I should stand still. She said that I needed to prepare myself to get inside of them, coax manhood from them, spark their genius, and remind them (over and over again) of their brilliance. I became a mother during 9/11, my sons came of age during #BlackLivesMatter, and they are navigating college in the Age of COVID-19. I have mothered them through the storms of racism, White nationalism, and White supremacy. I am not as courageous and fearless as I am going to be, but I am also not as frightened or as naïve as I used to be.

When my sons were little, I used to get up at night to check on them to make sure that they were still breathing. I would stand at the door of their room, and I would silently give thanks to them for choosing me to be their mother. I used to sit by their bed at night and read them poetry, telling them that they were the hope and the dream of our family. I would say to them how they were the descendants of enslaved men and women who chose to survive because they wanted them to live. I would say that they did it because they loved them even though they knew that they would never meet them. When I kissed them good night, I would whisper in their ear that they were diamonds and that my job, as their mother, was to brush off the dirt so that their brilliance and fire could shine through. I sheltered them, nurtured them, probably spoiled them because that was how my daddy raised me. He told me that I was brilliant and gifted. He treated my childhood paintings like they were prized Catletts and my poetry like Maya wrote it. He allowed me to make mistakes, to fall, and to find ways to get back up. He used to tell me that when I fell (at this point, he would always laugh because I was always falling), I needed to make sure that I fell on my back because if I could look up, then I could get up. My father's parents survived Jim Crow so that he could protest during the Civil Rights Movement so that I could grow up in a world without color restrictions, and my sons could one day be judged only by the content of their character.

In my mind, I believed that I was doing everything right until the day that George Zimmerman was acquitted of murdering Trayvon Martin. It was this moment and the subsequent launch of the #BlackLivesMatter movement that changed our household. I realized that instead of sheltering them, I should have been preparing them; instead of spoiling them, I should have been schooling them. It was the moment when I realized that I was raising two Black boys in the same racist world that my father was raised in, the one that he thought he had changed. It was at that moment that I became the #Blackmommyactivist and dedicated myself to helping to co-create a world where my sons would be safe. Ella Baker once said, "Until the killing of Black men, Black mothers' sons, becomes as important to the rest of the country as the killing of a White mother's son, we who believe in freedom cannot rest until this happens." This quote was a daily reminder of why I was fighting and why I had to win. My sons and I became activists, marching together, protesting together, trying to carve a new way forward together. They learned how to be both courageous and fearless.

We started keeping a list—adding to it daily—of every unarmed Black person who had been killed by state-sanctioned violence. At night, we would go out to the backyard and say their names. It was our small way of remembering them, of seeing them, of speaking their names into the wind so that they would not be forgotten. In the aftermath of 9/11, my sons learned how to be cautious and aware of what was happening around them. During Black Lives Matter, they learned how to be *racebrave*, so that they could confront and call out racist behavior, and they could pivot when they were being mistreated. They learned how to move forward in dangerous situations even when everything in them was telling them to stand still. And now, amid the "Age of Corona," they are learning how to be still and listen to themselves. They are becoming the young men that my family had always dreamed they would be: brave, fearless, beautiful, and brilliant. They have finally become my family's tomorrow.

About the Author

Karsonya "Kaye" Wise Whitehead is a professor of communication and African and African American Studies, the founding executive director of The Karson Institute for Race, Peace, & Social Justice at Loyola University Maryland and the host of the award-winning radio show Today With Dr. Kaye on WEAA, 88.9 FM. She has received the John Lafarge Award, which recognizes an individual who establishes coalitions to advance positive change, initiates difficult dialogues, and embodies activism in support of the long, blessed freedom struggle; the Vernon Jarrett Medal for Journalistic Excellence for her outstanding reporting on the impact racial reckoning has had in helping to close social/racial wealth gap for Black people in America; and the Regional Edward R. Murrow Award for Excellence in Diversity, Equity, and Inclusion.

She is the author of four books, including *RaceBrave: new and selected works*; *Notes from a Colored Girl: The Civil War Pocket Diaries of Emilie Frances Davis*, which received both the 2015 Darlene Clark Hine Book Award from the Organization of American Historians and the 2014 Letitia Woods Brown Book Award from the Association of Black Women Historians; and *Letters to My Black Sons: Raising Boys in a Post-Racial America*. She is a K-12 master teacher in African American history, an award-winning curriculum writer and lesson plan developer, and an award-winning former Baltimore City middle school teacher.

Dr. Whitehead is the former national secretary for the Association for the Study of African American Life and History (ASALH) and the current national President of the National Women's Studies Association. Additionally, she writes a bi-monthly column, "Conversations with Dr. Kaye," for the Baltimore *AFRO* newspaper based upon her deep ethnographic study within the Black Butterfly neighborhoods of Baltimore City. She is also one of the most sought-after keynote speakers in the country, having given over 500 keynotes worldwide. Dr. Kaye is a wife and mother of three children.

Apprentice House is the country's only campus-based, student-staffed book publishing company. Directed by professors and industry professionals, it is a nonprofit activity of the Communication Department at Loyola University Maryland.

Using state-of-the-art technology and an experiential learning model of education, Apprentice House publishes books in untraditional ways. This dual responsibility as publishers and educators creates an unprecedented collaborative environment among faculty and students, while teaching tomorrow's editors, designers, and marketers.

Eclectic and provocative, Apprentice House titles intend to entertain as well as spark dialogue on a variety of topics. Financial contributions to sustain the press's work are welcomed. Contributions are tax deductible to the fullest extent allowed by the IRS.

To learn more about Apprentice House books or to obtain submission guidelines, please visit www.apprenticehouse.com.

Apprentice House
Communication Department
Loyola University Maryland
4501 N. Charles Street
Baltimore, MD 21210
Ph: 410-617-5265
info@apprenticehouse.com • www.apprenticehouse.com

Printed in the USA
CPSIA information can be obtained
at www.ICGtesting.com
LVHW011118290923
759461LV00003B/65

9 781627 204873